ONE JEWISH BOY

Stephen Laughton

One Jewish Boy was first performed at the Old Red Lion Theatre, London, on 11 December 2018.

ONE JEWISH BOY

Stephen Laughton

The Company

JESSE	Robert Neumark-Jones
ALEX	Asha Reid
Director	Sarah Meadows
Producer	Ed Littlewood
Associate Producer	Liv Edmunds
Designer	Georgia de Grey
Composer	Benedict Taylor
Lighting Designer	Lucy Adams
Stage Manager	Heather Christie
Assistant Director	Katerina Constantinidou
Set Build	Lee McFadyen
Graffiti	Hannah Lawrence
Movement	Tina Barnes & Rachel Harper

BIOGRAPHIES

JESSE | ROBERT NEUMARK-JONES
Stage credits include: *King Arthur* (Story Pocket Theatre); *Bang Bang* (John Cleese/Made in Colchester); *The Tempest* (London Theatre Workshop); *Wolf Pack: Text* (VAULT Festival); *The Deep Blue Sea* (Drama Centre); *The Seagull* (Vakhtangov Institute, Moscow); *The Dangers of Tobacco* (Solo Festival); *Palmland* (Sheffield Crucible); *Stop, Look, Listen.* (Big Smoke Productions); *Kiss Me and You Will See How Important I Am* (Sunday's Child).

TV/film credits include: *Resting* (Turtle Canyon Comedy); *Spotless* (Tandem Communications); *Grange Hill, Hope and Glory* (BBC Television).

Robert is also a stand-up comedian and three-time Edinburgh award winner.

ALEX | ASHA REID
Stage credits include: *Graceful* (RADA Studio/Rosemary Branch); *Inside Pussy Riot* (Les Enfants Terribles); *Biggest Tarantino Fan in the World* (VAULT Festival/Arcola); *Edinburgh Test* (Pleasance/Old Red Lion); *Stay Happy Keep Smiling* (Jermyn Street); *I Found Joy in a Hopeless Place* (Hackney Showrooms); *Money Womb, Hacked* (Theatre503); *A Third* (Finborough); *Scarlet* (Southwark Playhouse); *Electra* (Old Vic); *Cross Purpose* (Crypt Gallery); *Medea* (The London Theatre); *The Hate Play* (Box Clever); *Miniaturists: The Interval* (Arcola); *Courting Drama* (Bush); *The Tempest* (Watford Palace); *Lord of the Flies* (Broadway Theatre); *The Magpies The Wolves* (Tristan Bates/ Pleasance); *The Beggar's Opera* (Regent's Park, Open Air).

Film credits include: *Into Me See, Face The Camera & Smile, House Hold, Gemma's Wedding, Puzzled, White Collar, Weird Love.*

Web series: *Nutritiously Nicola.*

DIRECTOR | SARAH MEADOWS
Sarah is an award-winning director and part of The Old Vic 12 2019. Sarah was nominated for an Off-West End Award for Best Director for *Screwed* (in collaboration with Out Of Joint) by Kathryn O'Reilly at Theatre503, and has worked across the UK, Europe and the USA. Sarah started her career in Manchester and worked as an Assistant to the Executive Producer and Artistic Director John McGrath (National Theatre Wales, Manchester International Festival) at Contact Theatre. Sarah directed across the north-west and worked at theatres such as the Library, The Lowry and Bolton Octagon, before relocating to London. Recent credits include: *The Talk* (Associate Director; UK tour); *The Fear of Fear* by Stephanie Ridings (Warwick Arts Theatre); *Alkaline* by Stephanie Martin (The Park Theatre); Assistant Director on *The Real Thing* by Tom Stoppard, directed by Stephen Unwin (UK tour, including Cambridge Arts Theatre/The Rose Kingston/Bath Theatre Royal; autumn 2017); *Summer in London* by Rikki Beadle Blair (Theatre Royal Stratford East); *The Texas Taxman* (musical comedy; Luke Courtier/Arcola/VAULT Festival/RADA festival; winner of the Comedy Award, VAULT Festival); *Pig* by Tim Luscombe (The Vaults, Waterloo); *Where Do Little Birds Go?* by Camilla Whitehill (Old Red Lion/UK tour/VAULT Festival/

Edinburgh Festival, Underbelly; The People's Choice Award, VAULT Festival); *Ile La Wa* by Tolu Agbelusi and Apples & Snakes, UK tour 2016); *Screwed* by Kathryn O'Reilly (Theatre503); the comedy *The Very Perry Show* by Kate Perry (comedy; San Francisco International Arts Festival); *Mr Incredible* by Camilla Whitehill (VAULT Festival and Edinburgh Festival 2016; Award for Outstanding New Work, VAULT Festival); *You* by Mark Wilson (Brighton Festival/VAULT Festival; winner of the Argus Angel Award, Brighton Fringe Award for Theatre, and The Fringe Review & Pick of the Festival Award, VAULT Festival).

Sarah is Co-Artistic Director of Longsight Theatre.

WRITER | STEPHEN LAUGHTON

Theatre credits include: *The Biggest Tarantino Fan in the World* (Arcola/VAULT Festival); *6equence* (JW3 R&D); *Run* (Bunker/VAULT Festival/Southwark Playhouse); *Screens* (Theatre503); *Nine* (Arcola); *Marina Abramovic Is Staring At Me* (Railroad Playhouse, NY/Cell Theatre, NYC).

TV credits include: *The Hobby* (Three Tables); *Doctors* (BBC TV); *Black Hill* (Lime Pictures); *Forward* (Blacklisted Films); *Tumble* (Double M Films).

Film credits include: *RWD/FWD* (Fully Focussed/GOOD Agency/ Restorative Justice Council; nominated for a Drum Content and Charity Film Award).

Stephen has produced a range of critically acclaimed film, theatre and TV productions: projects include the Academy Award shortlisted *Unknown White Male* and BAFTA and RTS award-winning *Tottenham Ayatollah*. Stephen co-directed a short-film, *Recompense*, which screened at the BFI and was an official selection for the New York Independent Film Festival, where it won Best Actor, Best Actress and Best Directorial Debut in the Short Film Category.

PRODUCER | ED LITTLEWOOD

Ed is currently producing *A Good Enough Girl?* (a co-production with Greenwich Theatre and Nutshell Theatre); *Handfast* (a Nutshell Theatre and Byre Theatre co-production); *At Your Leisure* (with Room 2 Manoeuvre as part of VisitScotland's Year of Young People 2018); and *A Joke* with Tony Cownie, Neil Murray and John Kielty. His production *Hector* successfully toured the UK with a London transfer (Ambassadors Theatre).

Past productions and partnerships include: Théâtre Sans Frontières; Creation Theatre (*Henry V, Lion, Witch and the Wardrobe*); *Plutôt la Vie By the Seat of Your Pants* (national tour/IPAY/Philadelphia International Children's Festival/ Imaginate Festival); *Paper Doll Militia* (LoopsEnd; VAULT Festival/Manipulate Festival); *Room 2 Manoeuvre* (Watch iT!; Made in Scotland Programme/ Almeida/Without a Hitch – Finland/Luxembourg/UK tour); Nutshell Theatre (*Allotment* ; Fringe First winner; UK tour,106 performances; *Thread*; Fringe First winner; UK tour, co-production with Assembly/ONFife).

ASSOCIATE PRODUCER | LIV EDMUNDS

Producer credits include: *Evolution HMS Comedy* (Canal Cafe/Edinburgh Fringe).

Associate Producer on *Marina Abramovic is Staring at Me* (Railroad Playhouse, NY/Cell Theatre, NYC).

TV: Gemporia TV (Sky channel 646, Freeview Channel 30), Rocks and Co productions (Sky UK, Freeview UK , Italy and Germany).

Writer: *Doreen* (web series).

PRODUCTION/STAGE MANAGER | HEATHER CHRISTIE

Heather Christie is a freelance stage and event manager with over eight years of experience in theatre, music and events. Heather has worked at venues such as Polka Theatre, King's Head Theatre, Park Theatre, Southwark Playhouse and Rose Theatre, and thoroughly enjoyed the fast-paced festivals such as VAULT Festival and Edinburgh Fringe Festival. Most recently Heather has been pursuing immersive theatre, credits including The Crystal Maze Live Experience, Myriad Productions, Boomtown Fair Festival and has worked with SPECIFIQ on several productions.

Heather is delighted to be rejoining Stephen again for his second play after working on his debut *Run*. She would like to thank her parents and brother for all their support.

COMPOSER | BENEDICT TAYLOR

Benedict Taylor is an award-winning composer and solo violist. He is involved with a number of higher education institutions, giving composition, improvisation and performance lectures at the Royal College of Music, City University, Royal Holloway, Goldsmiths College and York University. He is the founder/artistic director of CRAM, a music collective and independent record label, and published by Manners McDade Composer Publisher, London.

Benedict's work has featured with festivals, venues and organisations including: BBC Late Junction, BBC Hear and Now, Film London, Rotterdam Film Festival, Royal Court Theatre, BBC Arts Online, Berlinale, TriBeCa Film Festival, London East End Film Festival, Edinburgh Fringe Festival, Theatre503, London, Venice International Film Festival, BFI London Film Festival, VAULT Festival, London Contemporary Music Festival, Bike Shed Theatre, Third Man Theatre, Jazz en Nord Festival, Aldeburgh Festival, The Barbican, Cafe Oto, Royal Albert Hall, Southbank Centre, BBC Radio 3, BBC Radio 2, and Radio Libertaire Paris.

The composer for over a dozen features films, Benedict's recent projects have included *The Hungry*; original horror series *Ghoul*, *Maunraag* (monologue); award-winning film *The Bright Day*, and *Oysters*.

Benedict writes extensively for new theatre, composing for a number of award-winning contemporary plays. Recent theatre work includes: *Fireworks & The Djinns of Eidgah* (Royal Court); *Mr Incredible*, *You* and *Where Do Little Birds Go?* (Longsight).

www.mannersmcdade.co.uk/composer/benedict-taylor/

PRODUCTION DESIGNER | GEORGIA DE GREY

Theatre design credits include: *Rails* by Simon Longman (Theatre by the Lake); *Alkaline* by Stephanie Martin (Park Theatre); *Our Town* by Thornton Wilder (North Wall Arts Centre); *If We Got Some More Cocaine I Could Show You How I Love You* by John O'Donovan (Project Arts Theatre Dublin and tour/Old Red Lion); *Superhero* by Richy Hughes, Joseph Finlay and Michael Conley (Southwark Playhouse); *Spring Storm* by Tennessee Williams (North Wall Arts Centre); *Incident at Vichy* by Arthur Miller and *Caste* by T.W. Robertson (Finborough); *The Listening Room* by Harriet Madley and *Birthday Suit* by David K Barnes (Old Red Lion); *Erwartung* by Arnold Schoenberg and *Twice Through the Heart* by Mark Anthony Turnage (Shadwell Opera at Hackney Showroom); *Sister* by Alex Groves and Rebecca Hanbury, (Spitalfields Music Festival/Ovalhouse); *Best Served Cold* by Cordelia Lynn (The Locker, VAULT Festival); *The Last Five Years* (Tobacco Factory, Bristol); *The Last Days of Mankind* (Bristol Old Vic); *The Lonesome West* (Alma Tavern, Bristol) and *Pericles* (Redgrave, Bristol).

Georgia was the finalist for the Linbury Prize for Stage Design 2013, and winner of National Student Drama Festival Set Design Award at the Edinburgh Fringe Festival, 2009.

LIGHTING DESIGNER | LUCY ADAMS

Lucy Adams is a London-based lighting designer. She regularly collaborates with ThisEgg, having designed *Goggles*, *Me and My Bee*, *UNCONDITIONAL* and *dressed.* for the company. She's also worked with BREACH Theatre on *It's True, It's True, It's True*, Barrel Organ on *Anyone's Guess How We Got Here*, YESYESNONO on *[insert slogan here]* and Haley McGee on *Ex-Boyfriend Yard Sale*. Her lighting design for new writing includes *Tumulus* by Christopher Adams, directed by Matt Steinberg, *A Hundred Words for Snow* by Tatty Hennessy, directed by Lucy Atkinson, and *Skin A Cat* by Isley Lynn, directed by Blythe Stewart.

ASSISTANT DIRECTOR | KATERINA CONSTANTINIDOU

A young newcomer in theatre with a fine art and film background, *One Jewish Boy* is Katerina's first AD role in theatre. Her film and TV work includes, runner on award-winning films, *18* and *Drawn out*; and shadow AD on series 5 of *Luther* (BBC). Katerina joined Fully Focused in 2017 where she is the content creator of their award-winning youth media brand: MYM: Million Youth Media.

The Old Red Lion Theatre first opened its doors in 1979, and is now one of London's oldest and most loved fringe theatre venues. We are the Off-West End home of exceptional, ambitious and challenging theatre, ranging from world premieres of new plays to acclaimed revivals of significant productions from throughout history.

We support the UK's most exciting artists at crucial stages of their careers, presenting work that challenges our audiences and connects us to communities rarely given the opportunity to be seen on stage. Our mission is to nurture and present the very best of new, emerging theatrical talent. Esteemed artists including Abi Morgan, Joe Penhall, Kathy Burke, Stephen Daldry, Penelope Skinner and Nina Raine are just a few who had their early work presented on our stage, and this list grows each year.

The Old Red Lion Theatre has an unparalleled reputation across Off-West End theatre for staging challenging, ambitious work, and as such a significant number of our productions have transferred to the West End and Off-Broadway. We were the home to Mischief Theatre's premier of the now Olivier award-winning *The Play That Goes Wrong* before it transferred to Trafalgar Studios in 2013, toured the UK, and found its new home in the heart of the West End at the Duchess Theatre.

Other recent productions staged at the Old Red Lion that have transferred into the West End and beyond include the world premiere of Arthur Miller's first play *No Villain*, Ned Bennett's revival of Phillip Ridley's *Mercury Fur*, Moses Raine's *Donkey Heart*, and Naomi Sheldon's *Good Girl* (Trafalgar Studios); *Mrs Orwell* (Southwark Playhouse); *Kissing Sid James* (London and Off-Broadway) and *The Importance of Being Earnest* (Theatre Royal Haymarket).

Artistic Director and Theatre Manager: Katy Danbury
Executive Director: Damien Devine
Managing Director: Helen Devine
Bar Manager: Dylan Cole

ACKNOWLEDGEMENTS

The seeds of this play were once again sown at Courting Drama at the Southwark Playhouse earlier in 2018, so I want to thank Ryan Forde Iosco and Mathew McQuinn for asking me back and getting this journey started. The version we did was a whole other thing, but it was a hugely important stepping stone to this play, so a HUGE thank-you to Maud Dromgoole, Lauren Cooney and Olivia Ross. I love that our baby gave birth to this baby.

The creative team on this play have been incredible and it's been great to cement previous collaborations – Asha Reid (you basically always have a role), Heather Christie (so lovely to have you back!), Lucy (you've got through half of Playdate now – I want all the others lit by the end of next year!); work again with old friends – Liv and Ti (I love you both, you're two of my best friends and it's so wonderful to still be making shit together all these years after drama school!); and start whole new relationships… (Robert – you're my only Jewish boy, Ed – don't ever leave me; Georgia and Benedict – I'm so bowled over by what you've created, have been a fan from afar so it's wonderful to finally work with you; and Katerina – it's wonderful to work with someone right at the start of their career, you've been excellent, thank you.) I really can't thank you all enough. Your excitement, encouragement, talent and hard work has been amazing, and I've loved making this with you. Extra special thanks to Sarah, you're brilliant and not just a favourite director but a favourite person… You've made me laugh, you've challenged and pushed what this play can be, and you've kept me sane. I'm so glad we got a project up together. I hope we get to do more.

John, Matt and Sarah Liisa at Nick Hern Books – it's always lovely publishing a play with you.

To Playdate – Dave Ralf, Isley Lynn, Chris Adams, Poppy Corbett, Vinay Patel and Sarah Kosar – you're my spine. Thank you for the love and support and the fun.

Nick Quinn, Alfie Coates and The Agency team. Thank you for looking after me.

Katy and the ORL team, you've been behind this from the start, your faith and confidence in me, us and this project has been just super. Thank you.

Luke Johnson, The Mackintosh Foundation, Jan and Mark Bloomfield. Thank you so much for all the production support.

To Anoushka Warden and to Aaron Nathaniel for all the PR help… thank you!

HUGE huge really big thanks to Dan Simon and the team at Interim Spaces for their generosity, support and the use of their lovely rehearsal room at Pophub Leicester Square.

Sam Hayes, Sarah Sigal, Olivia McFadyen, Tina Barnes, Amanda Leigh Owen and Paul Bloomfield. You're my favourite people. I love you.

LM. You saved my life. This is for you. I can't ever thank you enough.

S.L.

ONE JEWISH BOY

Stephen Laughton

Love, love will tear us apart again.
Love, love will tear us apart again.

Joy Division

Characters

JESSE
ALEX

They are twenty in 2004, thirty in 2014, and thirty-four by the time we reach 2018.

Jesse is Jewish.

Alex is mixed race.

Note on Text

The usual dots, dashes, slashes for interruptions, broken thoughts, changes of gear, etc.

This text went to press before the end of rehearsals and so may differ slightly from the play as performed.

2018. A lounge in Walthamstow Village, London

A mural takes over the entire wall.

Boxes. No furniture.

ALEX *is awkwardly hovering.*

JESSE *aiming for* (*likely failing at*) *conciliatory…*

JESSE. But you're good, though?

ALEX. I guess.

JESSE. You look well.

ALEX. I look like Hillary Clinton dipped in Elton John.

JESSE. I don't know what that means.

ALEX. Glitter. My hair. No make-up.

You look nice / you always look nice.

ALEX. No I don't.

JESSE. Can I – (do anything?)

ALEX. You look like shit / too…

JESSE. Charming.

ALEX. Have you slept?

Are you my mum…?

ALEX. Here we go.

JESSE. What does that mean?

Beat.

ALEX *brandishes a large envelope.*

ALEX. Don't have long…

> JESSE *just stares at it.*

> Sorry.

JESSE. She's still sleeping…

ALEX. Your mom said she can pick her up later.

JESSE. You spoke to my mum?

ALEX. About an hour ago.

JESSE. I've been trying to call her all morning…

ALEX. She's taken your nan to the doctor.

> Her knee's all swollen up or some'ing…

JESSE. She didn't say she was taking her tonight…

> *Long beat.*

ALEX. Got a pen?

> JESSE *walks off.*

JESSE. Somewhere.

> *Beat.*

ALEX. Didn't think you were moving…?

JESSE (*absently, still looking for a pen*). It's a *family* home.

ALEX (*doesn't take the bait*). Do we need to talk 'bout selling?

JESSE (*slightly too aggressive for a pen*). I can't find a fucking pen!

ALEX. I've got a pen, Jesse.

JESSE. Of course you do.

ALEX (*roll of the eyes*). You want to make this difficult?

JESSE. I'm not making anything –

> *He takes the envelope. Ceremoniously takes out the document.*

Intensity as he reads the first page.

Beat.

ALEX *watches.*

JESSE *throws it down on to the floor.*

Irreconcilable differences...?

ALEX. Thought it was the –   JESSE. Name three.

Why?

JESSE. Name three of our *irreconcilable* differences, Alex...

ALEX. I'm not doing this –

JESSE (*cuts her off*). *Because you can't.*

ALEX. Stop it.

JESSE. It's so *official.*

ALEX. It's a line on a bit of paper.

JESSE. Rip it up.

ALEX. No.

JESSE. *I dare you.*

ALEX. Jesse –

JESSE. Alex...

ALEX. *Jesse.*

JESSE. Alex.

ALEX. What you doing?

JESSE. I thought we were saying one another's names...

   ALEX *shakes her head – she just can't...*

   She crosses to the window.

   Picks up the Chanukiah... absently picks at the wax.

   (*Watching.*) Stay for candles if you want –

ALEX. Why?

JESSE. Should've seen Poppy's face last night.

ALEX. I missed her.

JESSE. Spellbound…

ALEX. You take a photo?   JESSE. I'll send you the video
                                              if you like.
Thanks.

Puts the Chanukiah down.

JESSE. I feel like our differences could well be reconciled if we
just had a –

ALEX (*interrupting*). I don't know why this is a surprise.

JESSE. – conversation.

Maybe cos you know… it's a slightly overcast but a
nonetheless lovely Shabbat morning and you're having
breakfast with your lovely wife and you're a bit excited
about the lovely weekend you had planned ahead and as
you're passing the grapefruit juice to your *lovely* wife who
just gave birth to your lovely daughter you're suddenly
presented with a barked Jesse, Jesse – I want a divorce…

ALEX. That's not what happened…

They both let it hang. Beat.

We're completely / toxic… We've been at it like *Brangelina*
for months…

JESSE. We just had a baby…! It's a – Brange-fucking-lina…?

ALEX. I'm not sure why I –

JESSE. Cos Brad Pitt is a narcissist, philandering pothead who
slapped his kid about on a plane…?

ALEX. Well, I nearly said Johnny Depp / and Amber…

JESSE. *Wife-beater* Johnny Depp…?

ALEX. I'm Johnny Depp. Okay? *I'm Johnny Depp!*

JESSE. There's a really good chance we wouldn't be divorcing if you were actually Johnny Depp.

ALEX (*smiles*). Oh really…?

JESSE. For shit… that is one bromance I would fully consummate…

ALEX *breaks the smile and the eye contact first.*

Beat.

ALEX. Did you get your solicitor / to –

JESSE. I trust you…

ALEX. Jesse, you need / to get a –

JESSE. How complicated can it be?

Freedom. Check. Baby. Check.

House. Checkmate.

ALEX. That's not fair we said / you'd stay in the house anyway –

JESSE. I don't have a solicitor…

ALEX. Your dad's / a –

JESSE. I'm not letting my dad look at my divorce papers…

ALEX. Why?

JESSE. He already hates you.

ALEX. I get on really well with your dad.

JESSE. He does whatever my mum tells him, so…

ALEX. Well your mum answers my calls…

Beat.

…*so*…

JESSE. It's fine. If this is what you want…

Beat. Looks at her – is this what she wants?

Where do I sign?

ALEX. We can't even agree on where to live!

JESSE. You just hate London. / We don't even have to live in London.

ALEX. I don't hate London

I just hate all the people *in* London.

JESSE. And you think taking her to Paris is going to be any better…?

ALEX. What's up with Paris?

JESSE. They shoot Jews in supermarkets in Paris. They shoot Jews in Jewish schools in Paris. They burn old Jewish women in their dirty fucking Jew flats. *In Paris*.

ALEX. Well it's not like she looks particularly Jewish –

JESSE (*interrupting*). Great… so I'm the problem.

ALEX. No –   JESSE. Take me out of the
                                             equation –

That's not what I'm –

JESSE. Please don't go to Paris.

You haven't lived in Paris for –

ALEX. My dad is in Paris.

JESSE. My dad's in Highgate!

ALEX. I don't know / why that's –

JESSE. I thought we were having a dad-off?

ALEX. NO ONE NEEDS YOUR SHIT RIGHT NOW.

Beat.

JESSE. I'll do whatever you want.

I'll live… wherever you want.

ALEX. Paris?

JESSE. You've haven't lived in Paris since you left uni.

ALEX. It's where my dad is. It's where my dad moved. It's where the only surviving member of my family –

JESSE. *We're your family.*

ALEX. Just post them to me when you've signed them.

She starts gathering her things.

JESSE. Do you want me to wake her?

ALEX. I need to go.

She starts walking off.

JESSE. I don't want to post them…

ALEX. So what do you want to do / Jesse?

JESSE. Stay married…

She shakes her head, despair.

We started this together we should at least end it *together.*

She crosses, touches him. Reassuring.

ALEX. It's not because I   JESSE. Don't…
don't –

He takes her hand…

JESSE. We can make this work.

They're close. Both teary.

ALEX. We keep saying that…

Almost kiss.

The baby cries.

Beat. They peel away.

Stare. ALEX breaks it.

I wanna see Poppy.

ALEX *leaves*. JESSE *sits*.

(*Offstage*.) It's okay my darling, Mummy's here…

JESSE *listens, as Poppy settles*.

His heart breaking as we watch.

ALEX *walks back in*.

JESSE. I er… I was talking to Joan. Next door… the old –

ALEX. I know who Joan is.

JESSE. Yeah… she was in the garden… asking about the dog.

You. Poppy…

ALEX. That's nice.

Is she okay?

JESSE. Sure. Yeah…

I'm carrying the recycling and she starts moaning about the council… Feels a bit let down by them. Voted for them. First time in a long time. Wasn't worth it before she's a *Socialist… haven't had a Socialist Party in ages*.

That Tony Blair wasn't a Socialist. He should never've had the Party asks if I'm voting for 'em and I say not this time. I've always voted Labour, but I can't do it this time…

Oh, you're a *centrist*. Like it's a swear word. She says.

I tell her I wouldn't go that far but that I'm worried about anti-Semitism in the Party…

And you know she's never gonna have that… It's not real anti-Semitism, she says. There's no *real* anti-Semitism. She says. So, I tell her, *slowly*, that it's real… That it's very. Very. Real. That there are thousands of complaints, there's a Met Police investigation.

She's shaking her head. No, she says. It's all made up, she says. It's the *Jews*.

There it is. The Jews are making it all up.

Want to bring down Jeremy…

Do you know – I tell her – do you know that Jews in Britain have mainly been, historically been Labour supporters? *They're not though. Not really. She says. They're not REAL Socialists.*

Love their money too much.

Why they're all the bankers!

I'm saying sorry but it's not an apology, more an actual, *are you fucking serious, lady…?*

They don't like Jeremy because he's a Socialist, she says, think he'll take their money away!

And I just blurt it, cos frankly by now, just fuck her.

You know I'm Jewish…? You know that don't you?

I I I didn't know that my darling, she says. I didn't know.

And I feel upset, I tell her, I feel sad to hear you believe these things, that you really think thousands of Jews are lying.

That you think that all these Jews are dishonest and manipulative…

Do you really think they're lying?

And she locks eyes, this little old woman who I speak to every day –

Who I've helped, checked in on, worried about…

She locks eyes with me, and without a hint of apology, feeling, care or anything other than cold hard resolve, she says… Yes.

Yes, they are.

Beat.

ALEX. She's an old woman…

JESSE. So that's okay?

ALEX. What can she –   JESSE. It's exactly that kind
                                              of shit.

ALEX. I have to go.

She starts to make her way out.

JESSE. Don't leave me please don't leave me with all this
I love you so much Alex and I love our baby and our dog and
I don't I don't I don't want to end our marriage I love our
marriage I love you I love the way you make me laugh and
you're really hot and the way you smell and your hair I love
your hair and you're so beautiful and I really miss the way
you snore actually I used to find it really –

ALEX. Can you stop.

JESSE. Just.   ALEX. Please.

Please.   *I can't Jesse.*

They're both emotional. Fighting it.

ALEX. I have to leave.

I have to –

Because Poppy.

2012. A hotel balcony overlooking the East Village, New York

City skyline in the background. The Chrysler shining bright, up off Lexington Avenue.

JESSE *is vaguely phone-scrolling. Smoking from a vape.*

He's in bed shorts and a superhero T-shirt.

It's late. 2 a.m. late.

Drizzle.

Long beat as JESSE *listens in silence for a while before* ALEX *enters in an oversized T-shirt.*

She watches him.

After a few moments, ALEX *takes the vape from him. Inhales. Passes it back.*

JESSE. The sound of the rain is perfect.

ALEX. Come back to bed.

JESSE. Don't you think it's the perfect noise?

   Not all romantic and shit, just as noise, acoustics, chaotic rhythm, the odd car… the noise from the street.

ALEX. Jazz.

JESSE. Where's the jazz?

ALEX (*taps her head*). There is always jazz…

   Beat.

   It's freezing. Are you not freezing?

JESSE. I like it.

   She picks up a blanket from one of the benches. Wraps it around herself.

   I'm basically moon-bathing.

ALEX. You've got a healthy glow…

Beat. He smiles. She's about to sit opposite…

JESSE. What you doing? Come here.

She does, snuggles in to him. He pulls her closer, kissing her head as he does.

ALEX. You okay?

JESSE. Pensive.

ALEX. With your posh words.

JESSE. Pensive's not posh…

ALEX (*shrugs – nothing*). You wanna fuck?

JESSE. We're in New York so I guess we're vaguely obligated…

ALEX. That why you're up?

JESSE. Did I wake you?

ALEX. You weren't there.

JESSE. I didn't want to wake you.

ALEX. Well done…

JESSE. Sorry.

ALEX takes the vape. Inhales. Passes it back. He inhales.

(*On his out breath.*) You can see in that window over there.

ALEX. You're perving on the guests…

JESSE. It's a dude.

ALEX. You sure you're not bi?

JESSE. That's it.   ALEX. I wouldn't mind.

Beat. He shakes his head, she's an idiot…

ALEX. I don't like waking up without you.

JESSE. I'm waiting for the Benylin to kick in.

ALEX. Exactly how much Benylin?

JESSE. Enough.

ALEX. What's enough?

JESSE. It's quiet isn't it?

ALEX. What's enough, Jesse?

JESSE. Not enough to worry about.

    You think you'd hear more stuff though...

    We're in the East Village.

ALEX. It's two o'clock.

JESSE. It sold me as the city that never sleeps...

    Beat. He's an idiot...

ALEX. What you down about?

JESSE. I never said down.

ALEX. You never have to.

JESSE. Nothing. Really.

ALEX. Ah. That.

JESSE. Honest... I'm just...   ALEX. *Nothing really* is the
                                    worst.

    The pits...

ALEX. It sucks.

JESSE. It sucks balls.

ALEX. One of the seven circles of hell.

JESSE. I'm Jewish, we don't believe in hell.

ALEX. You don't believe in hell?

JESSE. Patriarchal Christian fabrication contrived solely to establish a ruling clerical elite to manipulate, divide – women/the poor/infirmed/sexuality spectrums, et cetera, and dominate.

ALEX. Isn't that all religion?

JESSE (*nods*). Also taxation.

Beat.

ALEX. Ennui…

JESSE. Now who's got the posh words?

ALEX. Je suis bilingue…

JESSE. Why is your French so shit? Didn't you used to live in Paris?

ALEX. Fuck you. I'm fluent.

He considers. Smiles.

Are you down…?

Considers. Smiles.

JESSE. Probably.

ALEX. We can fuck if you want.

JESSE. I feel a bit sick actually.

ALEX. What you eat?

JESSE. I tried to vomit before but I just retched a bit…

ALEX. I'm fully prepared to punch you in the stomach if you need…

JESSE. Thanks?

ALEX. That's how much I love you.

JESSE. That's probably quite sweet.

She grins. She is.

ALEX. What you reading…?

JESSE *presents the phone – it's the Rightmove app.*

JESSE. You know a studio in Greenpoint costs six-fifty?

ALEX. You want to move to Brooklyn?

JESSE. I feel like it's safer for Jews in Brooklyn.

ALEX. What about the mixed-raced woman?

JESSE. You'd be fine.

ALEX. Why?

JESSE. Cos you –   ALEX. Cos I look white?

    Well I wouldn't put it that –

ALEX. You know how infuriating and bullshit the perception of
white fucken privilege – it's offensive. Don't say that to me.
I'm mixed race.

JESSE. But people don't always know that you're –

ALEX. And people don't always know that you're Jewish. And
then they do. And then every single bit of that white fucken
privilege just goes… And you know how that feels – you
know yesterday?…

JESSE. Yeah?…

ALEX. When I went to the 711, on wotsit and I picked up this
magazine – a black hair magazine – the security guard
clocked it… suddenly made sense with my hair and my
features but my skin – he just followed me round –

JESSE. That was probably cos you're hot.

ALEX. That does not make it any better – because it's okay to
keep telling me keep telling me how good I look? Because
it's okay to say to someone – well done on your face…?
I mean cheers mate but it had nothing to do wiv me…

JESSE. Yeah. It's fucking bullshit.

ALEX. It is fucken bullshit.

JESSE. And we're gonna rise up against those fuckers…

ALEX. Yes we are…! And then we're gonna smash white privilege.

JESSE. And the patriarchy.

ALEX. Fuck the fucken patriarchy.

JESSE. Fuck them all… who wants to spend six hundred and fifty thousand dollars on a studio in Brooklyn anyway?

ALEX. A little bit…

JESSE. I think I'm a bit obsessed with Rightmove.

ALEX. You think?   JESSE. It's like Tinder for
                                    married people.

    We're not married.

JESSE. Yet…

ALEX. *Yet*.

JESSE. Get married if you want…

She considers.

ALEX. Only if we can honeymoon in Washington.

JESSE. It's not quite Cuba but I'm listening.

ALEX. Prince. June.

JESSE. We're not getting married in June!

ALEX. Oh you've decided?

JESSE (*laughs, nods*). My favourite chats are the ones when you don't really say anything.

ALEX. Isn't that all of them?

    ALEX *looks at the window* JESSE *was looking through and nods*.

    Oh, he's back.

JESSE. What do you think they're saying?

ALEX. They're watching TV

JESSE. Think it's porn…?

ALEX. No…

JESSE. That is fully porn…

ALEX. It's Netflix and chill at best…

JESSE. I'm way too old for Netflix and chill.

ALEX. *Salut*…

JESSE. I want a Virgin bundle and commitment.

ALEX. Less STDs.

JESSE. Fewer.

ALEX. I'm from Peckham. It's fine.

JESSE. Ohmygod, Amy at work got crabs.

ALEX. Shamey Amy?

JESSE. How do you think she got the name…?

ALEX. I think getting crabs at this point in life would be well grim.

JESSE. Totally.

But Aids is way grimmer.

ALEX. And now you're joking about Aids.

JESSE. There's no shampoo for Aids.

ALEX. Lovely…

JESSE. We can go to Washington if you like.

ALEX. I'm in.

JESSE. You're not the only Prince fan in the room…

ALEX. No?

JESSE. I love Prince.

ALEX. Name three Prince albums…

JESSE. *Batman*.   ALEX. That don't have
                                    a superhero, a year or
                                    a colour in the title.

She takes the vape back.

ALEX. It's proper pissing it down isn't it?

JESSE. It's nice.

It was nice before watching you dozing.

ALEX. Because that's not weird.

Smiles. Drift off again into a long beat.

JESSE. I realised we missed candles.

ALEX. Oh shit. Yes. Happy Chanukah! You want to light it
    now?

JESSE. Can you be bothered?

ALEX. Fun fact. I can always be bothered.

JESSE. Noted.

ALEX. I love Jew Christmas.

He goes inside.

ALEX *in thought.*

She wraps the blanket tighter.

Leaves it a moment. Looks after him.

Moves to where he was sitting. Picks up his phone.

Unlocks it.

Scrolls.

Is looking off every now and then.

Taps as she reads.

Her reaction: Bingo!

Beat as she reads. Then…

Her reaction: Heartbreak.

Lets the phone drop in her hand a little.

Exhales deeply.

Looks off.

Quickly locks and replaces phone.

Moves back to where she was sitting.

Pulls the blanket further up around herself.

Beat as she fights tears.

JESSE *walks back out.*

Immediately over-breezy…

JESSE. You're cold…

ALEX. I'm fine.

He sets up the Chanukiah.

Two candles – one on the far right of the Chanukiah. And he holds the other.

Helps me feel…

He stops for a second. Beat.

Then he lights the Shamash candle.

JESSE. Ba-ruch A-tah Ado-nai, E-lo-he-nu Me-lech ha-olam. A-sher ki-de-sha-nu be-mitz-vo-tav, ve-tzi-va-nu le-had-lik. Ner shel Cha-nu-kah.

Ba-ruch A-tah Ado-nai, E-lo-he-nu Me-lech Ha-olam. She-a-sa ni-sim la-avo-te-nu ba-ya-mim ha-hem bi-zman ha-zeh.

He lights the candle, looks at the light through his fingers.

ALEX *watches on.*

Ba-ruch A-tah Ado-nai, E-lo-he-nu Me-lech Ha-olam.
She-heche-ya-nu, ve-ki-yi-ma-nu, ve-higi-a-nu liz-man
ha-zeh.

ALEX. Happy Chanukah...

He kisses her.

JESSE. Your gift's inside...

ALEX. I hope it's a pony.

JESSE. Maybe it's Prince tickets.

ALEX. Then I'll marry you.

He smiles, starts humming 'Maoz Tzur' quietly to himself.

Beat, as he does.

You know we met three years ago today?

JESSE. Today today?

ALEX. Saturday today.

Beat. He considers.

JESSE. How do you even remember that?

ALEX. I'm perfect...

JESSE. *Oui.*

You're wrong though.

Well technically you're absolutely right...

But you're wrong.

ALEX. It was the first night of Chanukah.

JESSE. Chanukah moves. Hebrew calendar...

Lunar. It was later... so we're a couple of weeks off...

ALEX. Fucken moon.

JESSE. But it's our Jewy-versary and that's important too.

ALEX. So, we should celebrate...

JESSE. Have we got any champagne?

ALEX. I'm from Peckham.

JESSE. I don't know if that means we have champagne or not…

ALEX. It means I'm too cool to drink champagne.

He leans down and kisses her.

JESSE. I was reading about Gaza…

ALEX. Why are you reading about Gaza…?

JESSE. Cos every time it kicks off in Gaza…

ALEX. That was months ago –

JESSE. I needed some distance before I could bear to look at it…

ALEX. Fair.

JESSE. And I was reading about those boys…

ALEX. What boys?

JESSE. Like three fifteen-year-old boys old American settler boys who were kidnapped and murdered –

ALEX. You can't murder fifteen-year-olds –

JESSE. In fairness some Palestinian kid was killed first and this was a –

ALEX. Someone just needs to lock them all in a room until they sort it out –

JESSE. Well yes… but then like months later, like all these synagogues and mosques and stuff came together and had vigils for the all the kids that had been killed…

ALEX. That's beautiful…

JESSE. It's emotive… sure –

ALEX. It's more than emotive…

It's *affecting*…

The solidarity of the human spirit.

JESSE. It shouldn't take a pyscho, and the murdering of innocent kids to –

Unify.

ALEX. Well there are nutters everywhere…

JESSE. Well yes.

ALEX. People are capable of some well fucked-up shit…

I was in Cannes once…

JESSE. Fancy.

ALEX. I was working an event, and then this one day I went down to the beach cos I had the late shift and I'd clocked this guy – on the boulevard and he looked harmless enough. And I found a nice spot on the beach… but cos I'd spotted him again, I chose a spot that was between this family and then a group of mates smoking weed.

JESSE. I can see where this is going?

ALEX. You think?

And I'm lying down, on my front and I feel a shadow you know which is weird cos there is not a cloud in the sky and I look up and he's there and I'm thinking why are you behind me, but I don't say anything cos I never say *anything*. I'm just thinking stay over there and perv from afar mate and I turn back over, on my front and the next thing you know, completely out of nowhere cos I haven't even spoken to the twat, he just licks me.

JESSE. What?

ALEX. Told you…

JESSE. That's fucking –

Where did he lick you?

ALEX. My bum…

JESSE. On your –   ALEX. Yeah.

What were you wearing?

ALEX. It shouldn't matter what I was wearing. I could lie here naked if I wanted to.

JESSE. No I mean... skin, or did he just lick the material or what?

ALEX. Skin.

   My bum. He licked my bum.

JESSE. Like the side or between the –

ALEX. The side but still it doesn't –

JESSE. I mean fucking hell Alex... What did you do?

ALEX. Nothing.

   Not a fucken –

   I looked around and no one even gave a shit cos no one saw and he just gave me this grin and it became clear to me I had nobody – so I just –

JESSE. Why are you telling me this?

ALEX. Cos we're talking about nutters Jesse...

   And I I know it feels sometimes that it's discriminate but I wonder if there's just something really fucken...

   I dunno...

   Sick.

   In the human soul... so women, gays, I dunno... different ethnicities, Jews... I mean anything that isn't white and male is just –

JESSE. I hear you. And on one level you're absolutely right.

   But I'm not sure it's the same thing.

   It is discriminate.

   There's a special level of hatred –

ALEX. Yes. The hatred of the 'other' is pretty fucken –

JESSE. Kind of but still every seventy years...

ALEX. Seventy what?

JESSE. Bang.

Pograms. Expulsions... The Shoah.

It's just the start.

No other people in history have ever been so hated, so
constantly...

| Like every third | ALEX. That's what I'm |
| generation... | talking about – |

Time to fuck up the Jews.

And I was talking to my therapist and –

ALEX. Wait... you're in therapy?

JESSE. Isn't everyone?

ALEX. No.

JESSE. Maybe you should think about it...

ALEX. And why do you even need therapy?

JESSE (*they've been here before*). Jew shit.

ALEX. That's not a thing, Jesse.

JESSE. It's kind of a thing...

Beat. She smiles, raised eyebrows.

Okay. Fine.

Inherited trauma.

| ALEX. Bullshit... Inherited – | JESSE. I totally feel inherited |
| | trauma. |

Isn't that a bit self-indulgent...?

JESSE. It depends how you're defining.

ALEX. *Indulgently...*

JESSE. Is self-indulgence a bad thing?

ALEX. What is wrong with you?

JESSE. Clue. It's not a bad thing.

It's pretty selfish.

JESSE. It's not like self-obsession for instance... and I feel like it's really important we make the distinction –

ALEX. And I feel like it's time for bed.

JESSE. – that in and of itself, self-indulgence is probably pretty healthy.

ALEX. Inherited trauma feels pretty self-indulgent.

I mean, how far do we go back?

JESSE. Jew shit is an actual thing Alex. And you need to be sensitive to it.

ALEX. The potato famine? And I'm sensitive to it.

JESSE. Oh come on –

ALEX. Okay.

Slavery.

JESSE. Sure.

Yes. Slavery – slavery was like yes the worst and you would be / fully justified in –

ALEX. But I refuse to let any of that get in the way of –

JESSE. And that's brilliant and I wish I was able to –

ALEX. Look, so I'm thinking about leaving work.

I want to go it alone...

JESSE. What?

ALEX. Start-up. Consult as I build up.

JESSE. We're talking about –

ALEX. I've always wanted my own events company.

It's time.

JESSE. Wait. Slow down.

ALEX. Now he wants to slow   JESSE. Weren't we saving for
down.   a deposit?

The beat is miniscule but it's there.

I've worked it out and I think that within –

JESSE. It's gonna be more difficult to get a mortgage if you
don't have a regular salary, Alex.

ALEX. I think it might be better.

JESSE. You do?

ALEX. I think within two years I could be doubling my income.

JESSE. Two years? I don't wanna live in that shitty shared
house for two more years –

ALEX. The amount of money we pay for contractors – there are
people doing the equivalent of my job for two, three times as
much.

JESSE. And they're just gonna what? Let you leave and then
hire you as contractor?

ALEX. They've opened up voluntary redundancy. I've been
there seven years, we're looking at between fifteen and
twenty grand. It's enough to get set up and build a client base
and most of them will come with me… so –

JESSE. I'm not sure Alex…

ALEX. You don't have to be.

JESSE. There's a lot for us to think about before you –

ALEX. It's my career.

JESSE. That's not fair. It's *our* life…

ALEX. I'm signing it all off when we get back.

JESSE. And you were gonna tell me –

ALEX. I'm telling you…

JESSE. Okay…

    Okay…

ALEX. I need you to support this.

    It's exciting.

    It's next level…

JESSE. No. Next level. Yeah.

    I'm gonna piss.

ALEX. Sexy.

JESSE. Among certain sub-communities…

    He gets up… Starts to walk inside.

ALEX. We should go out… Celebrate.

JESSE. Out…?

ALEX. When was the last time we went out?

JESSE. Outside?

ALEX. To a club…

JESSE. I'm nearly thirty!

ALEX. Let's go out. Throw some shapes. Get all geometric.

JESSE. I've got a blister…!

ALEX. I thought you had a headache…?

JESSE. Is a blister sexier…?

ALEX. We're in New York!

JESSE. Someone told me once that *Snow White and the Seven Dwarfs* is about cocaine. You ever hear that?

ALEX. No…

JESSE. It's supposed to be about the seven stages you go through or something…

ALEX. Where do you find this shit?

JESSE. On coke. Apparently.

ALEX. Do you have coke?

Can we have coke?

JESSE. Come on.   ALEX. I miss cocaine.

I miss cocaine.

ALEX. I'm a much better person on cocaine.

JESSE. Same.

ALEX. Shall we call *Harry Weed New*?

JESSE. My old pot dealer is called Harry.

ALEX. I know.

His entry is Harry Weed New in your phone.

JESSE. Don't go through my phone.

ALEX. Too late.

The beat is microscopic, but it's absolutely there.

JESSE. Alright, let's go out... I would quite like to see you all sexy and geometric.

She stares, hard... then jumps up...

Finds a track on her iPhone. Hits play.

It's 'Raspberry Beret' by Prince.

She dances.

And is indeed, sexy and geometric... And just really fucking cool.

ALEX. Well don't just stare at me...

Come on...

She dances again.

He joins. Then.

He stops dead. Is suddenly really upset.

JESSE. My um. What I wanna say… Is –

My love for you is. Is so deep and all-consuming and. Furious.

ALEX. Jesse…

JESSE. It's so much bigger than me. And it terrifies me Alex.

It has me at the throat.

ALEX. Are you trying to leave me?

JESSE. Sometimes I think that's why I should.

ALEX. O-kay…

JESSE. But I I'm I I I'm just I'm mainly terrified that it will destroy us.

ALEX. Who is she?   JESSE. In the end.

JESSE. What?

ALEX. You're going to lie?

JESSE. What?

ALEX. You can tell when someone is about to lie because when you ask a direct question they say 'what' to buy themselves thinking time. So –

JESSE. I'm not trying to –

ALEX. Who is she Jesse?

JESSE. She's just. I just. I just. I fucked someone.

ALEX. I know you idiot.

ALEX *throws the nearest thing to her at him. It's his phone.*

JESSE. It was just a fuck. I'm sorry. I'm so sorry. You're better. Not better. I prefer you. I'm sorry. I love you.

ALEX. I don't care that you fucked her. If that's what we're doing here I'm fine with that. I care that you didn't fucken tell me.

You're fine? You're fine with this?

ALEX. Did you use protection?

JESSE. Of course. Of course I did.

Will you marry me?

You're like the best thing that ever happened to me and ever since we met I have just felt so much like so much safer like actually safer with you... I do... When I'm with you... Like like like like the fascism right it doesn't arise just arise in an existing democracy... it has to be placed it has to be to... tested... so –

No. Listen. Just. Don't you see how that's happening right? It doesn't just arise... You have to test it. There's testing. And we're seeing it. Now. *Populism*. And I can't not I I I can't not be with you Alex... Like no one else... no next girlfriend or ex-girlfriend... Just you. When I think of that world... when we've

ALEX. Because, if I get gonorrhoea cos you didn't bag it there will be a shitstorm.

What are you doing? Get up you ridiculous – best thing that ever happened to you? If I'm the best thing that ever happened to you why are you fucking other women in the first place? If I'm the best if you feel safe with me. And it's fine... like I said... it's fine if that's what we're doing here – it's fine I mean is that what you want to do here are we open now? And if we are open now does that change if you're proposing and if you were thinking about proposing to me, why do you think framing it like –

Have you actually taken cocaine?

This is really fucken creepy actually because

been exposed to that that savagery... then then then you have to marry me.

actually you think you love me but I'm not sure you do because actually you just have me on some weird. Fucking pedestal –

JESSE. No I don't.

ALEX. Yes you do. And that's not love, that's just setting me up for a fall actually.

JESSE. I need you to marry me.

ALEX. You think I'm going to say yes?

JESSE. Please say yes.

I'm. Sorry.

I just love you so much.

Please say yes. Please.

ALEX. You're seriously proposing right now?

JESSE. I don't know your ring size.

2016. A street in Trappes, Paris

After midnight.

Run-down social housing.

The walls are covered with street art. Good street art – murals, etc. Not just shitty graffiti tags.

JESSE is sitting up against a wall. The mural behind covering its entirety.

He sits on the ground, out-to-holiday-dinner casual. There's a couple of empty bottles.

JESSE is tipsy, a little wound up, smoking.

Long beat. ALEX rounds the corner. Flustered, a little more dressed up.

She is not happy when she spots JESSE.

Beat… They lock eyes.

JESSE. So, he's a cunt.

ALEX. I mean, don't hold back…

JESSE. Fuck off, Alex.

ALEX. Fuck off, Jesse!!

    You know how important this meal was!

    You can't just storm off like that…

JESSE. And there is no way in all hell he is coming to the wedding.

ALEX. We have been looking. Literally.

JESSE. Or his child bride.   ALEX. E-ve-rywhere for you.

    She is no way more than twelve…

ALEX. She's like twenty-two.

JESSE. Is that why she wanted to go to fucking Miniature Land anyway?

ALEX. Stop it.

JESSE. That is the shittest theme park I have ever been to!

ALEX. Jesse.

JESSE (*bad French accent*). *Disneyland is so obvious… You must see a real Parisian theme park…*

ALEX. *Stop it*.

JESSE. You know she's fucking…

ALEX. We need to go.

   Jesse.

JESSE. I fucking hated her.

ALEX. Jesse!

JESSE. Someone needs to drown the bitch.

ALEX. That is not acceptable language.

JESSE (*carrying on over her*). Oh piss off…

   Preaching.

ALEX. Do you know how dodgy is it out here?

JESSE. Well if we're using prior levels of…

   Hostility as a –

ALEX. This is not Élancourt –

JESSE. I mean what even was that?

ALEX. We need to go.

JESSE. Israel… and Jewish are completely. Fucking. Separate –

ALEX. This is the *banlieue. You've come into the banlieue.*

JESSE. I take it back actually. She's the cunt.

ALEX. *Stop it*.

JESSE. Like how many times do I have to say to *everyone*…

> I HATE IT TOO. IT HAS NOTHING TO DO WITH ME
> AND IT SICKENS ME TO THE CORE.

> I AM NOT A BLANKET ZIONIST.

ALEX. Stop shouting.

JESSE. I am a diaspora Jew. I have very little… in fact *nothing*
to do with Israeli foreign policy.

ALEX. Well it's not quite foreign.

JESSE. Are you serious right now?

ALEX. Can we go please?

JESSE. Oh I'm sorry, should I just *prendre la fuite, madame*…

ALEX. What? I don't know what you're saying…

JESSE. *Prendre la… jump… shall I just jump, princess…?*

ALEX. You're not using it correctly…

JESSE. No one asked for a French lesson –

ALEX. I am not responsible for any of this…

JESSE. Why can't you just defend me…?

ALEX. Why can't you just keep your mouth shut…?

> *Deliberate beat. He glares.*

> See… even now…

> Can't help yourself.

JESSE. I didn't say   ALEX. You know exactly –
anything…!

> Just go back to your boyfriend.

ALEX. He's not my –

JESSE. Any more.

> He's not your boyfriend any more.

ALEX. Is that what this is?

JESSE. No, Alex no. That is   ALEX. Are you jealous?
    not what this is.

    (*Talking over her.*) No I'm no – fuck you...

    This is a reaction to being called a Nazi.

ALEX (*talking over him*). The banlieue is not safe.

    There is a burnt-out car –

JESSE. *A fucking. Nazi.*

ALEX. He didn't –

JESSE. Don't you dare –

ALEX. He didn't say the word Nazi –

JESSE. He literally just said. In front of you.

    Like this close...

    Like so close you could probably feel his hard-on –

ALEX. Don't be crass.

JESSE. Fine. His goyshe fucking pig breath.

ALEX. You are acting like a real prick. You know that?

JESSE (*talking over her*). *Jews should know better because of
    what happened in Germany.*

ALEX. That's not calling you a Nazi though is it?

JESSE. He's not the brightest tool... It wasn't exactly subtle...

ALEX. He's really upset.

JESSE. *Awwww poor ickle fingy.*

ALEX. You need to dial back the aggression –

JESSE. Oh I'm sorry do you feel threatened?

ALEX. A little. Actually.

JESSE. Oh do one…

ALEX. I don't like this colour on you.

JESSE. Are you actually having a fucking laugh?

ALEX. Okay. I'll see you at   JESSE. Could you be any
the hotel.   more of a cliché right
                                                         now??

She turns. Walks…

JESSE. Alex…

ALEX. I'm getting a cab.

JESSE. I'm sorry…

I'm just –

Alex.

She stops.

ALEX. It's rough here. We need to go.

JESSE. It's fine.

ALEX. It's not fine. There are kids all down the way, looking for people like us to fuck over.

JESSE. You're *fine*. C'mon.

I'll use my Nazi fucking…

Magic –

…to protect you…

ALEX. Your Nazi magic?

Beat. They both try not to laugh.

JESSE. I could not think of a word.

ALEX. So you landed on magic?

JESSE. I'm really upset and it sounded way sharper in my head.

ALEX. I'm engaged to Harry Potter.

JESSE. Don't take the piss.

ALEX. No… sorry. You're right.

Don't want you to zap me with your Nazi magic.

JESSE. You're a ridiculous human being.

ALEX. Me?

Beat. Long beat.

JESSE. I can't even go on holiday without some ape giving me shit about Benjamin Netan-fuck-you…

ALEX. Did you just make that up?

JESSE. Yeah, fully.

ALEX. Smooth.

JESSE. I am so fly right now, I could play Quidditch…

ALEX. You and your magic…

Knob.

What am I gonna do with you?

JESSE. My magic knob?

ALEX. We need to go. I'm getting an Uber.

JESSE. Wait. Is that my coat?

ALEX. Did you only just see it?

JESSE. I was reeling from the anti-Semitism.

ALEX. It was hardly anti-Semitic.

JESSE. I'm sorry. I love you.

But you don't get to call it.

Beat.

(*Shouts.*) Why is it so fucking cold?

ALEX. It's December? I don't know... The northern
hemisphere is closer to space?

JESSE. We live in London... My family are from the Shtetl.
I should be built for this shit...

ALEX. So what are you built for?

JESSE. I dunno...

Let's fuck off right now and find out.

ALEX. If it calms you down... I'm game.

JESSE. I feel like it's gonna be the same everywhere, though.

The whole world hates the dirty fucking Jew.

ALEX. You could go to Israel.

JESSE. I'm not going to *Israel*...

ALEX. Apparently you love it.

JESSE. Apparently...

But...

Likud...

And...

It's really hot.

And... I'd die.

And... if I didn't actually die my mum would be so worried
that I could potentially die at the hands of some crazed
militant Hamas toddler in a tunnel with a flame-throwing
teddy or just scorpions... actually... not terrorist scorpions –
that's not a thing... just actual insect scorpions, are they
insects? Scorpion scorpions. Little fucker scorpions with
claws and stings – them... So actually the the the sheer
nagging alone would end with my plunging from the top of
Mount Sinai.

ALEX. Which is in Egypt.

JESSE. Exactly. So getting my body back would be an absolute bitch.

ALEX. We established I do not like that word…

JESSE. We did. I'm sorry.

ALEX. We could go to America.

JESSE. They love the Jews in America.

ALEX. Shall I book tickets?

JESSE. Do it.

ALEX. I'm serious…

JESSE. Good. Cos, I'd follow you to the end of the earth.

She does Pyscho *with the knife and the noise*.

It's true.

I'm besotted with you.

ALEX. Just don't turn me into a dress.

Laughter.

Where in America?

JESSE. New York.

ALEX. Medium… LA.

JESSE. I hate LA.

Chicago.

ALEX. Florida.

JESSE. Did you not hear the bit where we talked about how I'm from the Shtetl. In deepest darkest fucking Arctic Russia. I will literally just burn.

Seattle.

ALEX. Chattanooga…

JESSE. What you call me?

ALEX. Stop it!

It's the capital of Tennessee.

JESSE. You'll find that's Nashville.

ALEX. *Fine...* I enjoy how it sounds.

But also, Nashville.

JESSE. DC. I could get my politics on.

ALEX. Too soon...

JESSE. I'm sorry.

ALEX. *It's the worst thing you've ever done...* We missed Prince!

JESSE. We were only a day late...

ALEX. Prince!

And, Washington is just Hollywood for ugly people.

JESSE. Well I believe we once established who was the good-looking one here.

ALEX. You're good-looking.

JESSE. Thanks.

ALEX. Mostly.

Beat. She sits.

Fucking Uber cancelled on me!

My dad spoke about Mum after you stormed off...

JESSE. Okay.

ALEX. It's my mum's memorial...

JESSE. When?

ALEX. January. Ten years...

JESSE. Then we should go.

Beat.

ALEX. I never noticed this church.

JESSE. That is one motherfucker of a spire.

ALEX. It looks like a really big penis.

JESSE. My really big penis?

ALEX (*tapping his forehead*). This one. Yes –

JESSE. Still got it.

ALEX. You know what they say…

Once you go white, nothing is right.

JESSE. When did you not go white?

ALEX. I don't actually see colour.

JESSE. Well it's suddenly quite apparent what you see…

She laughs.

I think you'll find the phrase you need to worry about is, once you go cut…

You'll find foreskins really quite disgusting actually.

ALEX. Well that just trips off the tongue, doesn't it?

JESSE. The foreskins?

ALEX. *Stop!*

JESSE. I'm sorry about tonight.

ALEX. Me too.

JESSE. It's okay… I love you…

ALEX. I think I should go to the memorial on my own.

Sorry.

Beat. He tries not to react…

JESSE. O-kay…

ALEX. I just think… To… To to spend some time with my
dad…

And to remember Mum and we can…

I don't know. Just be. Without having to worry about – just.
Just us.

He doesn't know me as an adult.

And he won't be around for –

Long.

And he should know me as an adult.

I think it's the right thing to do.

Just this once…

Long beat. JESSE *just manages to fight it.*

I hope you can understand that…

He smiles. Touches her.

JESSE. Wait…

ALEX. What now?

JESSE. Listen…

They listen.

Beat.

*We hear 'Fuck the Pain Away' by Peaches/2 Many DJ's – in
the distance.*

Can you hear that?

ALEX. I love this song. This song gives me goosebumps.

I've got goosebumps

JESSE. I've got itchy balls.

ALEX. Why do you ruin everything?

JESSE. Conflated sense of ego?

  Major mommy issues?

  I have no self-esteem and I'm desperate for approval...?

ALEX. Check check check.   JESSE. I don't fucking know.

  Oh my god Ibiza...

JESSE. Space?

ALEX. No! Stop.

JESSE. It was me, it was you! 2004 –

ALEX. No! You're such a weirdo!

JESSE. June! On the beach! We listened to this and smoked
  a spliff!

ALEX. No we didn't! You'd never do that anyway.

JESSE. I was twenty! I did it then. I was trying to impress you.

  You were off your face and you don't remember.

ALEX. Meant to be...

JESSE. I know. I kissed you goodbye.

ALEX. No you didn't.

JESSE. We listened to this.

  On the beach.

ALEX. No we didn't.

JESSE. What if it was me...?

ALEX. It was absolutely not you.

JESSE. I've always remembered you.

ALEX. You're full of shit...

JESSE. Wouldn't it be fucking beautiful if it was us...

ALEX. Well… yes…

But it wasn't…

JESSE. Like, beshert… meant to be… like fucking Romeo and Juliet.

ALEX. Romeo and Juliet die, you know that right?

JESSE. Whoa, Alex! Spoiler alert…!

ALEX. Oh god Beefa was nearly fifteen years ago…

JESSE. Twelve.

ALEX. Still.

Over thirty feels like a big deal.

JESSE. It's not forty.   ALEX. The end of youth.

That's forty-five.

ALEX. That's telling…

JESSE. Time to think about cracking on with the kids though.

ALEX (*re: her phone*). Why is Uber in Paris so shit, where the fuck is he going?

JESSE. Don't change the subject.

ALEX. I'm not changing the subject. I'm just getting us out of here which is what I've been trying to do for the past ten minutes. So really, you're changing the subject.

JESSE. Don't you want to have kids with me?

ALEX. My battery's gone. Can I have your phone?

JESSE. Wait.

Why don't you want to have kids with me?

ALEX. Stop being ridiculous. I'm trying to get us –

JESSE. No no no no no…

You're suddenly all like cagey and shit.

ALEX. I am not cagey… I'm ordering a cab.

JESSE (*half-joking*). Why don't you want to have kids with me, Alex?

ALEX. I want to go.

JESSE. Don't you want kids with me?

ALEX. We're in the middle of Murder Mile Paris.

This is not the time to talk about having a baby.

JESSE. I'm not going anywhere until you answer the question…

ALEX. So I'll see you at the hotel.

JESSE. This is really important actually.

ALEX. So is not getting murdered, mugged or raped.

JESSE. I can't marry someone who doesn't want my kids…

ALEX. I want your kids. Of course, I want your kids.

/ Can we go now please?

JESSE. So what's the problem? Like why was that so hard to say…? Like sometimes Alex, Jesus-fucking-Christ.

ALEX. Why are you getting upset again? I thought we –

JESSE. Yeah.

Slight beat.

Then you got all –   ALEX. I'm pregnant.

What?

Beat.

ALEX. Yeah.

JESSE. What?

Beat.

That's amazing. Ohmygod Al… that's brilliant.

ALEX. Is it?

JESSE. It's not?

ALEX. I can't take time off right now… the business is really –

JESSE. I can…

ALEX. And then –

JESSE. What?

>*Beat.*

>(*Laughing.*) What Alex…? It's not mine?

>*Beat.*

>I'm *joking*…

>*She shrugs.*

>It is mine right?

>Alex…?

2014. A kitchen in Hackney, London

Mess. Undecorated. Boxes.

JESSE. Close your eyes –

ALEX. Why?

JESSE. Cos I asked.

ALEX. I have a sense of smell –

JESSE. Why are you trying to ruin it?

ALEX. I'm not I can just –

JESSE. Close them.

ALEX. No –

JESSE. You're ruining it –

ALEX. But I can smell fish 'n' chips –

JESSE. How stupid do you think I am?

ALEX. Medium.

JESSE. Shut up and close your eyes.

ALEX. I missed you –

JESSE. Eyes –

ALEX. What?

JESSE. Close them –

ALEX. I have.

JESSE. I can see –

ALEX. They're closed!

JESSE. You're peeping –

ALEX. Kiss me.

JESSE. I'm going –

ALEX. Noooooooooo.

Kiss me. You're so handsome.

Kiss me… Come here –

JESSE. Eyes.

ALEX. I'd like to remind you that you have a beautiful woman throwing herself at you.

JESSE. More like a femme fatale trying to entrap me…

ALEX. I'll take that.

JESSE. Eyes *Alex*!

ALEX. Okay. Okay…

You better not do anything though.

I hate surprises.

Where are you? I'm opening my eyes.

JESSE. You won't get the present –

ALEX. I'm bored now –

JESSE. You're so juvenile.

Here you go.

It's a really nice bottle of champagne.

ALEX. That's not fish 'n' chips.

JESSE. I told you I was clever.

ALEX (*grins*). When?

JESSE. It's Krug.

ALEX. I can see.

JESSE. Vintage.

Well. 1984. The year we were born.

I've been saving it.

ALEX. Since then? – fuck we're old…

JESSE. Oi…

ALEX. Chilled too. You're so sweet.

Fish 'n' chips and champagne.

Kiss.

Look what we did Jesse… Look at our house.

JESSE. I mean… you did most of it…

ALEX. Potato po-fucken-tar-to –

JESSE. Can we do Chanukah?

ALEX. Is that today?

JESSE (*nods*). Did you unpack the glasses?

ALEX. I unpacked the record player.

JESSE. Is that all you did while I was out?

ALEX. Well I did a lot of thinking…

JESSE. O-kay…

ALEX. I actually have a bunch of life questions that I've been waiting to bring up…

JESSE. Important life questions?

ALEX. Well… Bread. Who decided it was a good idea to grind down some grass, add fungus, sugar and salt, water leave it then bake it… and then wipe the separated fat of cow mucus across it?

Who made that a thing?

And coffee?

We'll take this seed from this random berry. Roast it, grind it and pour hot water through it…?

JESSE. You are such a weirdo.

ALEX. These chips are really very good.

JESSE. I told you. So did you unpack anything else?

ALEX. Records.

His reaction.

Actually.

JESSE. Where are you going now?

ALEX (*re: champagne*). Give.

Come in here. I've got something I want to show you.

Sit there...

I was trying to find something to dance to before and I found this old record...

JESSE. Let me guess...

ALEX. Don't ruin it.

It's 'Hyperballad' by Björk.

ALEX has found this point in the record a hundred times before, it's about three minutes and twenty seconds in.

You need the / build-up –   JESSE. The build-up right –

She illustrates the bit she likes by singing along and kind of dancing at JESSE from the bridge section...

JESSE's seen it before and mouths the words right back.

Just before the song breaks to the instrumental at 4:05 we get a:

Wait for it... The best bit...   JESSE. The best bit.

JESSE pulls ALEX forward and kisses her.

I love this song.

She sits down on the floor next to JESSE.

They both stare ahead listening to the music.

JESSE takes a long swig of champagne, passes it. ALEX drinks.

After about a minute, as the music starts to wind down to the slow violin ending, ALEX *moves her head to the side, and then rests it on* JESSE's *shoulder.*

JESSE *smiles, his eyes glancing down at* ALEX.

JESSE *moves his head, so that his cheek is touching the top of* ALEX's *head.*

ALEX *looks up,* JESSE *looks down.*

JESSE. I love you.

It's not long before they have held hands. ALEX *closes her eyes.*

Smiles.

2009. Parliament Hill, Hampstead Heath

JESSE, *curled up, is having the shit kicked out of him.*

ATTACKER. You fucking parasite.

Kicking.

Hitler was right. He should have gassed the lot of you.

Throws a bottle, smacks him with a dog's chain.

You dirty fucking Jew…

2016. A street in Islington

ALEX *is heavily pregnant.*

JESSE *is eating a bag of chips.*

JESSE (*proffers bag*). Want a chip?

ALEX. I'm explaining woke.

JESSE. They're good chips.

ALEX. Are they woke chips though?

JESSE. Well I apparently don't know what woke is…

ALEX. I want the pickled onion.

JESSE. Absolutely not.

ALEX. Just a bite.   JESSE. No. No. No. No. No.
                                                No.

How about a skin layer?

JESSE. Oh please don't eat my pickled onion…

ALEX. You can have all the chips.

JESSE. I've been saving it.

ALEX. Less calories though.

JESSE. Fewer…

ALEX. I know, Jesse…

She winces.

JESSE. What was that?

ALEX. I just got a sharp –

JESSE. Okay okay okay… You can have the onion…

ALEX. That's not what –   JESSE. How sharp?

Sharp sharp.

What's the date?

JESSE. You're not due for ages…

ALEX. Well, I was a week early…

JESSE. It's at least three. I think you'll be fine…

Beat. He passes the chip bag over.

Enjoy your onion.

He pauses. Looks about. She tries not to rise.

ALEX. I can't handle the – (*Breathes through.*) grease.

JESSE. The grease is wonderful…

ALEX. I just got another… .

JESSE. What's it like?

ALEX. Like a weird twinge

JESSE. I think you're fine. You'll be fine.

You can walk… You're fine.

There's a moment as she takes that in.

I'm actually beginning to think my soulmate might be carbs.

ALEX. Well… maybe you can bother carbs with your incessant attempts at sexing…

JESSE. Erm… you're still my mistress. Actually.

ALEX. I think you'll find I'm your wife…

Although right now I feel like your heifer.

JESSE. Shut up you're stunning.

ALEX. Which is precisely what they do to heifers just before they slaughter them.

JESSE. Well, I just want to put this right out there, I enjoy you visually.

Pregnant you is hot.

ALEX. Well enjoy the visuals because we're never having sex again.

JESSE. Not on your life lady.

ALEX. Fine but you're having a vasectomy.

JESSE. My little boy penis was butchered enough in the first week of my life…

  I am not having a vasectomy.

ALEX. Do you remember that?

JESSE. Original trauma.

ALEX. Oh you and your traumas…

JESSE. Vaguely inherited when you unpack it…

ALEX. We are not going into inheri–   JESSE. I'm fucking with you. Literal no memory.

  Good.

  You never struck me as a chubby chaser.

JESSE. As, clearly the only feminist in the room –

ALEX (*talking through him*). This is called a street…

JESSE (*he doesn't stop*). – I feel like we need to unpack how problematic that is.

ALEX. As problematic as explaining feminism to me?

JESSE. Ow…!

ALEX. What?

JESSE. I just bit the inside of my cheek.

ALEX. You eat too fast…

JESSE. I don't…

ALEX. It's okay. *You're talking… You're fine…*

JESSE. You're not funny.

ALEX. I am. It's called karma. And you pronounce it, *ha*!

JESSE. You're all charm tonight.

ALEX. Can we sit down a minute…?

JESSE. Let's just get home. You've been on your feet all day.

If it's still a worry we'll –

He suddenly takes her arm. Forcefully marches her across the road.

ALEX. Owww –

What are you doing?

JESSE. Bloke there… Looks a bit –

ALEX. That hurt…

JESSE. Sorry. He looks a bit –

ALEX. What? A bit what?

Beat. Searching…

JESSE. Let's just go.

ALEX. No Jesse.

What the fuck was that?

JESSE. I feel like I've done something…

ALEX. It's not cool.

JESSE. What's not cool?

ALEX. Crossing the road when you see someone who's a bit – (*Air quotes on the bit.*)

Is not cool.

Beat. He stops. Indignation.

What?

JESSE. I'm not a racist.

Beat. Her glare.

JESSE. I'm not… but the demographic –

ALEX. There –

JESSE. What?

ALEX. Because the demographic has changed... I never had you pitched for a *Brexiteer*...

JESSE. There are *actually* all sorts of reasons people voted –

ALEX. Did you vote for Brexit?

JESSE. Can we just go home please...?

ALEX. Ohmygod Jesse, did you vote Tory?

JESSE. No of course I didn't I hate Tories... Darth Mayder is –

ALEX. But you didn't vote Labour and you keep going on about being rudderless lately and if you voted Brexit and I'm pretty sure you voted Brexit then why not just make the full leap to –

JESSE. I didn't vote Brexit.

ALEX. Liar.

JESSE. Don't call me a liar.

ALEX. Well I don't know what to believe.

JESSE. Are you serious right now?

ALEX. Well, the brown-looking man started walking towards us and you crossed over, so...

JESSE. There's been a marked change in the demographic of this part of Islington since 'austerity' and I'm speaking mainly about crime and not about colour because the fucking Tories are ruining this country by decimating our services. And frankly and I'm sorry but there is a left-wing argument for Brexit actually, because the EU is fundamentally undemocratic in fact it's already a neoliberal prison which locks in austerity for any nation that signs up... so it's possible to vote *Lexit* and not be a racist...

ALEX. Would you have crossed if he was white?

JESSE. Why would that matter?

ALEX. Because he looked like you?

JESSE. I'm not white.

ALEX. No?

JESSE. No!

> *Beat. She stares. Re: You're white.*

> You know full well that / Semitic and Caucasian are two distinctly –

ALEX. I know that you saw a man who didn't look like you and you crossed the road.

JESSE. He could've been anyone.

ALEX. I got attacked here once.

JESSE. What?

ALEX. By a white guy –

JESSE. *I'm not white!*

ALEX. He came up all – *Can I borrow your phone. My battery's died.*

JESSE. And if you gave it to him you're an idiot.

ALEX. He took it actually.

> Forcibly.

> After smacking me in the face.

> But I don't cross whenever I see a white guy.

> I mean imagine the… (*Zigzagging with her hands.*)

JESSE. I'm not white Alex.

ALEX. Would you've crossed the road if it was my dad?

JESSE. No. Don't be ridiculous. That's not what I'm saying!

ALEX. A lot of people Jesse. White people *Jesse*. Cross the road when they see my dad.

JESSE. I'm. Not. White.

ALEX. Well my mum's white…

So…

She shrugs.

JESSE. I don't know what you're saying…

ALEX. I'm saying like you're saying that people are fucken idiots and we all face it.

JESSE. Exactly…

ALEX. But this is new on you.

JESSE. What's new?

She considers. She doesn't rise to it.

What's new, Alex?

ALEX. It doesn't matter. I just wanna talk about something wholesome.

JESSE. Like broccoli?

ALEX. Or our daughter.

JESSE. Not long now.

ALEX. Hopefully a little longer though. It hurts.

JESSE. Stop worrying. I promise you. You're okay…

ALEX. Yes doctor.

I can't wait to meet her.

JESSE. Same… I've always wanted a little girl.

Which is weird cos all the guys I know want boys and all the women I know want girls which makes sense I guess…

ALEX. I kind of wanted a boy.

A gay boy actually cos they love their mums more…

JESSE. I know at least three gays who hate their moms.

ALEX. Wait.

Don't you hate your mum?

JESSE. No, piss off, she's just weird.

And a narcissist... .

But thank god we're having a girl though cos you are absolutely not making our son gay.

ALEX. Well... he can be gay if he wants...

JESSE. I mean, yes of course, but, there's a lot there...

ALEX. Such as...?

JESSE. Just the scene and stuff...

ALEX. But what does a lot there mean?

JESSE. Some of those guys are hardcore.

ALEX. I don't think they're any worse than the scenes we grew up on.

JESSE. Crystal meth –

ALEX. You don't think straight people take crystal meth?

JESSE. Are you accusing me of homophobia now?

ALEX. Of course not... I'm mainly just saying thank god for a girl really cos no one wants to –

She mimes scissors cutting as she bites down loudly on her teeth.

JESSE. What's up with –

He mimes scissors cutting as he bites down loudly on his teeth.

ALEX. Just –

JESSE. Just, what?

ALEX. Why are you always defensive?

JESSE. I'm not always anything.

We talked about this.

ALEX. I just said there's a bit of me that's relieved it's a girl.

JESSE. Because…

ALEX. Because I'm not sure I can do that to my little boy.

JESSE. Your hypothetical little boy won't feel it.

ALEX. They cut through his penis with a blade. Of course he'll feel it.

JESSE. Well, as a boy, whose penis *they* cut…

I'm telling you he won't.

ALEX. You just don't remember it.

JESSE. So what does it matter?

ALEX. I will.

JESSE. It's not your penis.

ALEX. Is it yours?

JESSE. Why do you always turn the question?

ALEX. I was reading that until they're three…

JESSE (*interrupting*). Oh were you reading? What were you reading?

Beat.

ALEX. It doesn't matter.

JESSE. No please.

Enlighten me.

ALEX. What are you doing?

JESSE. What are *you* doing?

ALEX. I hate it when you get like this…

JESSE. Well I hate it when someone takes it on themselves to goysplain the pros and cons of Judaism to me –

ALEX. Careful…

JESSE. I don't force my culture onto you…

She rolls her eyes.

What was that?

ALEX. Nothing.

JESSE. Don't roll your eyes...

I don't Alex... I do not force...

ALEX. Okay. Fine.

I mean...

You talk about it enough.

JESSE. What does that mean...?

ALEX. It's the basis of every example and every decision that you make.

JESSE. And you're telling me your upbringing and religious-secular beliefs do not inform your own process?

ALEX. No more than anyone else's...

JESSE. Exactly – you just notice mine cos it's 'other'.

ALEX. You're a nice educated boy from North London. How *other* do you think you actually are?

JESSE. I'm not gonna feel bad because my grandparents who escaped the Holocaust and came here with nothing worked hard enough for my parents to have an education. I'm not going to apologise for that. It's amazing. I'm proud / of them. They turned it around within a generation.

ALEX. I'm not asking you to feel bad, I'm asking you to consider whether your head start, from hard work or anything else, is really any more 'other' than the Jamaican-Irish Catholic Windrush girl from a council estate.

JESSE. Oh is that the girl who lives in the four-hundred-thousand-pound garden flat on Orford Road?

ALEX. I have worked really hard for that flat. I have made compromises and taken the kind of shit that would have had you reeling and I have kept my mouth shut consistently… at all the dicks and all the letches and the racists actually Jesse and the class bullshit and all of it… and have kept my head down and played the long game and worked really fucken hard and I have taken risks and put myself on the line in ways you couldn't even fucken imagine for that fucken flat.

JESSE. Well done, you.

ALEX. It is actually. Because unlike you Jesse, I don't have minted parents to bail me out when –

JESSE *licks his thumb and wipes* ALEX*'s nose.*

What are you doing?

JESSE. Wait you've got like a smudge on your nose and it's really cute –

ALEX. Stop it –

JESSE. I can't have an argument with you if you look really cute –

ALEX. I argue with you when you look cute all the time.

JESSE. Do you think I look cute?

ALEX. You can't just make a joke to sidetrack me whenever we're having a discussion…

JESSE. Do you think I look cute, though?

ALEX. You look beautiful.

JESSE. You do.

Her reaction. Relenting.

ALEX. Look, I'm sorry I said that I'm glad we're having a girl.

But I am… I'm sorry. I don't want to circumcise my son.

His reaction.

Oh come on… / we just –

JESSE. This is how it starts.

ALEX. What starts?

JESSE. A criticism here. A modification, a retraction…

Then you separate. Redefine a liberty.

Then before you know it –

ALEX. Don't you tire of this?   JESSE. We're redefining the
                                   International Holocaust –

JESSE. Yes actually. I do tire of the worry that yes… any day
now – they're coming for us.

ALEX *(frustration, rather than fury)*. WHO JESSE??? WHO…

JESSE. Take your pick! Every other religious group.

The far right – actually the not-far-off-the-centre left –

Jeremy Corbyn!

ALEX. Do I look like Jeremy Corbyn?

JESSE. You look worse because you look like you're on my
side /

ALEX. I AM ON YOUR SIDE.

JESSE. No you're not because EVERYONE –

Everyone Alex, everyone hates the DIRTY FUCKING
JEWS…

It never stops. And I'm scared Alex. I'm actually fucking
scared.

ALEX. Why do you think I hate you? I'm your… Jesse. I love
you…

JESSE *(carrying on)*. And I'm fucking sick of it. All the time.
That guy up there. Your dad / you have introduced me to like
twice because there are –

ALEX. Don't bring my dad into this.

JESSE. And because Jews do not fit traditional definitions of
marginalisation –

ALEX. What the fuck is a traditional form of marginalisation?

JESSE. Anti-Semitism places Jews as powerful, dominating, and privileged. So, if Jews are oppressors – nice. Educated. North. London. Boys. Then they cannot be included in intersectional coalitions, and their experience of oppression is erased.

ALEX. Speak English.

JESSE. Exactly. EXACTLY.

ALEX. Don't you see that part of the problem here is that you're standing there sounding like an academic fucken –

JESSE. You keep proving my   ALEX....essay!
point.

The accusation of white privilege plays exactly into that Jews equals the oppressor who controls your banks and your money and your media and your government anti-Semitic fucking – bullshit.

Like white privilege ever protected us from ANYTHING.

ALEX. I will scream.

JESSE. Then scream. Someone needs to fucking well scream.

ALEX. We're talking about circumcising my son.

JESSE. No we're not.

ALEX. Well maybe because nothing is ever a simple conversation with you.

JESSE. Loyalty. Oppression. Control and blood libel. / The four pillars of anti-Semitism.

ALEX. We're not talking about circumcising – ?

JESSE. Untrustworthy. Repressive. Dominating. And dangerous. That is always. Always the fucking accusation at the heart of anti-Semitism.

ALEX. I have never ever –

JESSE. You're doing it now… You're locating a run-of-the-mill custom right into the middle of blood libel, into the middle of dangerous –

ALEX. No I'm not –

JESSE. – and you can't help it because it's been drummed into you so fucking hard that there is a part of you that worries that I'm so fucking heartless that I would hurt my own fucking child.

ALEX. You're being ridiculous.	JESSE. Blood libel.

JESSE. So on a domestic scale it's kind of fucking shit actually and has stopped you ever quite trusting me but on a grand scale Alex… out there… On a grand fucking scale… that distrust in us leads right to the next Holocaust…

ALEX. NO IT DOESNT.

JESSE (*not stopping*). Because fascism, and this is a form of exactly that fascism, works on the idea of –

ALEX. Testing yes blah. Testing…

I was there when you proposed…

JESSE. You keep undermining me. Just listen!

Brexit has turned the tide on Islamophobia so now we need a new group… and the only other group that has faced major, historical hate.	ALEX. You listen. You're preaching to the converted Jesse… I don't really know why you're preaching to begin with actually.
Because you don't get it.	I can't do this every five minutes. I can't –

JESSE (*talking over her*). Hello, my name is Dirty Jew.

ALEX (*talking over him*). I get it better than anyone you know.

JESSE (*talking over her*). So Jeremy Corbyn refusing to accept the full International Holocaust Remembrance Alliance definition of anti-Semitism for instance is a test run…

ALEX. They accepted it!

JESSE (*talking over her*). After three months… to stave off a leadership challenge… it's not the same and it plays precisely into that split-loyalty idea, and then what? Down and down, further and further until we find history repeating itself. Expulsions. Pograms. Ghettos. The Holocaust. All over again. Enabled because Zionism is a swear word and the accusation of apartheid is the nuclear weapon.

I don't personally know any Jew who doesn't want a peaceful resolution to the Israeli-Palestinian problem.

I'm sure some exist, there are extremists everywhere, but to treat a whole community as if they all cheering on Netan-fuck-you is ridiculous.

It's anti-Semitic. Hate.

And it's the narrative… this vermin group is brutal, this vermin group is evil, this vermin group is not nought point nought one per cent of the British people, this vermin group is the secret dark power who killed your God and aims to enslave you.

This vermin group is dangerous. This vermin group has to go.

ALEX. We're talking about my hypothetical son.

JESSE. Your hypothetical son who you've been brainwashed to think will be abused by this very vermin group… a group not content with killing the children of Palestinians – *school bombings*, or Christians – *blood sacrifices*, even their own poor children – *circumcision* – aren't safe.

ALEX. I have not been brainwashed…

JESSE. I hear the shit you say –

ALEX. What?

JESSE. The micro-aggressions all the time…

ALEX. Are you serious-(ly) – ?

JESSE. And it's now at the point where I'm seriously considering whether it's actually just safer to move to Israel.

ALEX. We are NOT moving to Israel.

JESSE. There you go.

ALEX. Don't you dare…

JESSE. It's not your fault – it's why I let it go all the time, it's
    ingrained…

ALEX. So, I, your wife, the mother of your child, the woman
    who stood by you when you had an affair / is an anti-
    Semite…?

JESSE. The woman who jumped so fucking high at the chance
    of one-upmanship that she probably isn't actually the mother
    of *my* child…

ALEX. That was anti-Semitic?

JESSE. No that was just cunty.

ALEX. Fuck you, she's your child.

JESSE. Is she?

> *She tries to steady herself but the mounting pain she's been
> feeling is now searing. She can barely steady herself.*

   I'm just scared Alex. I'm really really just scared.

ALEX. I think we should call the doctor.

JESSE. It's nothing –

ALEX. Oh you're the doctor?

JESSE. It's a Branston Hicks.

ALEX. Braxton.

JESSE. Branston. Braxton.	ALEX. As in the singer.
Whatever…	Toni. Braxton.
It's phantom. Preparatory.	I know what a Braxton –

Toni Braxton?

ALEX. Are you seriously mansplaining this to me right now?

JESSE. Is that who they named it after?

ALEX. Of course not you fucken idiot.

JESSE. Don't call me an idiot.

ALEX. I didn't call you an idiot.

JESSE. I have ears.

ALEX. I called you a fucken idiot.

Actually.   JESSE. Nice.

It's not a Braxton Hicks.

JESSE. Why are you being such a bitch?

ALEX. Call me a bitch again… I dare you.

JESSE. I didn't call you a bitch.

I said you were being a bitch…

ALEX. It's the same thing.

JESSE. It's not the same   ALEX. *It's the same thing*.
thing –

Will you please stop riding my arse…

ALEX. Me? Mr *my-wife-is-an-anti-Semite*?

JESSE. You. Alex. Are not… a bitch.

But sadly. Today.

Borderline anti-Semitism actually aside…

You're being – I'm sorry but you are – a complete bitch.

She slaps him. Hard.

JESSE. Fucking hell Alex.

ALEX. I warned you   JESSE. Your ring just…

Call me a bitch again.

JESSE. We need to go home. Can you get an Uber?

ALEX. Stop telling me what to do.

JESSE. My battery died...

ALEX. Take me to hospital.

JESSE. My battery died...

ALEX. *Take me to a hospital.*

JESSE. It's a Bransto–

ALEX. Braxton.

JESSE. I DON'T CARE WHAT IT'S CALLED.

You're not going into labour. You're three weeks off.

Your water hasn't even broken.

You'd frankly be in a lot more pain than –

ALEX. Don't you dare tell me my body.

JESSE. You get a pass on most of your bullshit right now.

You're being ridiculous. And dramatic.

ALEX. What if there's a problem?

JESSE. Of course that's where you escalate...

You think I'm a mug?

Labour...?

ALEX. Just call a cab...

JESSE (*over her*). Like how perfect is your labour timed. I accuse you of some low-level unconscious racism and suddenly 'owwww... Jesse my waters broke...' Because you're trying to control and manipulate because you're always trying to control and manipulate so...

ALEX. FUCK YOU FUCK YOU FUCK YOU FUCK YOU FUCK YOU FUCK YOU FUCK YOU FUCK YOU FUCK YOU FUCK YOU FUCK YOU FUCK YOU...

JESSE. Whoa –

What the Jesus Alex…?

I'm just –

ALEX. No… you know what you are?

Actually –

The surge of pain rips through her… the contractions are coming with increasing frequency now.

JESSE. Why do I have to be something…

Why can't I –

ALEX. You're a snide nasty little brat.

JESSE. And you're a fucking bitch.

ALEX (*over him*). I don't like you.

I don't particularly fancy you.

I certainly don't trust you.

This constant CATASTROPHISING…

Oh my god just stop it…

You know I'm scared of you?

And you bore me. And you ruin everything.

Have you ever thought all this might not be because you're a Jew / but maybe cos you're a dick…?

JESSE. Don't call me a Jew.

A. Jew. Like I'm a thing…

ALEX. What are you then?   JESSE. Grow up.

It's fine I know what you are…

JESSE. You are making it very difficult –

ALEX (*she doesn't let him finish*). Every bit of love I have for you, you've taken away with your nasty attitude and your constant tantrums.

JESSE. Mine?

ALEX. How can I spend my life with you, how can I raise this poor bump with you, if I essentially can't stand being around you?

JESSE. Oh do one Alex.

ALEX. Yeah go on. Walk off.

Geezer...

JESSE. Cos this is worth staying for?	ALEX. Cos you're such a geezer!
	Dick.

Beat. He goes.

ALEX. You're a coward!

And we're done by the way.

AND FUCK YOU.

FUCK YOU JESSE.

She's been trying to hold in the pain but it's too much.

We are over.

WE.

ARE.

SO.

THROUGH.

She collapses against the wall.

Cries.

Pulls herself together as pain rips through.

Oh no...

No no…

Fuck.

She pulls her phone out as another contraction tears through her.

She swallows the scream but the pain makes her drop the phone.

She tries to bend down but can't as another contraction comes…

Jesse!

She unbuttons her bottoms… but it doesn't help.

Turns to face the wall, leans against it.

Jesse!

Screams as another contraction rips through…

2009. The Royal Free Hospital, Hampstead

JESSE *is in bed.*

ALEX *walks in.*

JESSE. Ohmygod –

ALEX. Hi.

JESSE. Hello.

ALEX. I hope I'm not –   JESSE. No. Come in.

  – invading am I?   Come in.

  I just wanted to see that you're –

JESSE. No. Of course. Wow. Come in. Sit.

ALEX. Sorry.

JESSE. Why?

ALEX. You don't mind me   JESSE. If I knew you were
  just –   coming.

  – turning up…   Baked a cake and all that.

  You bake?

JESSE. I don't know why I said that.

  Slight beat.

ALEX. It's good to see you.   JESSE. It's really lovely to
                      see you.

  How you doing??

JESSE. A lot better than last time.

ALEX. Good. So / how long are you –

JESSE. Thanks for the dog.

ALEX. Oh god no, it's fine… your mum came and –

JESSE. She said. I hope he was okay.

ALEX. He's adorable.

JESSE. He's a little shit.

ALEX. I like him.

JESSE. She said he wee'd on your sofa.

ALEX. It's fine. You're good.

JESSE. I can pay for the –

ALEX. I'm actually quite the dab hand with a bottle of Febreze, white wine vinegar and a scented candle.

JESSE. Thank you for finding him.

ALEX. Well… you're lucky I had my eyes peeled.

JESSE. And calling me an ambulance…

ALEX (*sing-song*). Jesse's an ambulance, Jesse's an ambulance.

Slight beat. He can't help but grin.

(*Shrugs it off.*) It's a funny phrase… isn't it? Keeping your eyes peeled…

JESSE. *What?*

ALEX. Think it hurts?

JESSE. I haven't really thought about it.

ALEX. Nor me.

How's your face?

JESSE. It hurts.

She touches it. Tender.

Proper stitches.

ALEX. Apparently scars are sexy.

JESSE. Apparently.

ALEX. You know they caught the guy.

JESSE. Mum said.

ALEX. Font of all knowledge that one…

You get your shit back?

He shrugs.

JESSE. So, I don't wanna be rude but…

ALEX. So don't be rude.

JESSE. I just wondered why you're here…

ALEX. That's not rude.

They're scoping each other out… not really saying anything.

I wanted to check you're okay.

JESSE. Okay…

ALEX. Is that weird?

JESSE. A little bit.

ALEX. Oh should I – ? (*Points to leave.*)

JESSE. Absolutely fucking not…

ALEX. Okay.

JESSE. Okay…

Still scoping each other out… not really saying anything.

Of course, you know what else is weird, don't you?

ALEX. Hit me…

JESSE. I mean the last person who did that –

ALEX. Fair. Yeah. Sorry…

Go on… I do not know what else is weird.

JESSE. Wind.

ALEX. Wind *is* weird.

How does that even happen?

JESSE. I want to say magnets?

ALEX. Check you, Einstein.

JESSE. Something like that.

ALEX. Big fuck-off magnets though.

JESSE. Huge.

ALEX. Vast. Interplanetary.

JESSE. Nebulonic…

ALEX. Is that a thing?

JESSE. I think it's probably electromagnetic waves.

ALEX. Isn't that just a fancy way of saying magic?

JESSE. I like magic.

ALEX. They been looking after you?

JESSE. It's a good hospital this.

ALEX. I haven't been in a hospital for ages…

He proper fucked up your face didn't he?

JESSE. Thanks…

ALEX. You wanna talk about it…?

JESSE. What's there to talk about.

Some gimp kicked off. Found out I was Jewish, kicked off some more…

Scared my dog. Smashed a bottle in my face and stole my shit.

You found me.

Fast-forward… and… Hello…

ALEX. Hello.

A seagull stole my pizza once and then dropped it on a baby…

It's nowhere near as bad as all this, but I felt awful cos I was torn between feeling really bad for the baby who was screaming cos baked cheese is –

Hot... and it was deep pan, so...

heavy...

...and wanting my lunch back...

JESSE (*smiles*). You're a dickhead...

ALEX (*grins*). I get a bit awkward. Sometimes...

The Jew shit is bad. I'm not trying to detract or anything...

Beat. She grins. They're close.

JESSE. Seagulls terrify me, like... serious.

ALEX. What do you think they're planning?

Beat.

JESSE. I mainly think that they're the foot soldiers for the general Dolphin Armageddon...

ALEX. Is that even a thing?

JESSE. More imminent and terrifying than the zombie apocalypse.

ALEX. I'm not sure I'd be good in a zombie apocalypse...

JESSE. No?

ALEX. Alien invasion... find me – I've got your back... but zombies...

JESSE. Don't worry... I'll protect you...

She lets it hang.

ALEX. I should probably be –

JESSE. Oh okay...

ALEX. Oh look at your little face...

JESSE. Sorry was that needy...

ALEX. Needy's fine.

I do have to go though. Work and –

JESSE. Okay.

It hangs.

ALEX. I haven't been in a hospital since, my mum died…

JESSE. I'm sorry…

You know that I don't know your name…

ALEX. Alex.

I'm Alex.

JESSE. I'm Jesse.

ALEX. I know who you are…

JESSE. Hi Alex.

ALEX. Hi Jesse.

2018. A bedroom in Walthamstow Village, London

It's about half an hour after the first scene.

JESSE is topless.

ALEX is drying herself.

JESSE. Are you okay?

ALEX. No.

JESSE. I just want to –   ALEX. Don't you dare thank
                                       me.

I wasn't going to thank you.

ALEX. Good.

I hate it when you thank me for sex.

JESSE. I've been thanking   ALEX. I know. I hate it.
you for sex for –

Why didn't you say?

ALEX. Sixty-nine per cent of spouses tell lies.

Eighty per cent of women lie to protect someone's feelings.

You're the teacher… work it out…

JESSE. Fucking hell Alex.

Beat.

ALEX. We shouldn't have done that.

JESSE. I just want to be clear that you pointedly said yes.

ALEX. Jesus Jesse, I'm not accusing you of rape!

JESSE. Shit can get grey when you're in this…

Purgatory…

So, I was… Deliberate.

About obtaining consent.

ALEX. I should go.

JESSE. Why?

ALEX. Because I want to go…

JESSE. I want to kiss your eyes and your lips and have you fall asleep on me and as you drift off make all sorts of small but important promises I'll keep forever

It's physically crushing but she manages to steady herself. Just.

Beat.

ALEX. I have an a– [ppointment]

JESSE. Don't you get that I really don't want you to go.

She puts on her shoes.

Do you really want to go?

She hesitates.

Don't go.

ALEX. I just need –   JESSE. What do you need…?

Beat.

I don't know… a cuddle… a shower…

He gets up.

Grabs a T-shirt.

Don't get dressed…

If we both get dressed it kind of ends the –

JESSE. So don't get dressed.

She sits. Head in hands.

He pulls her close.

They hold one another really tightly.

Long long beat as they cling to one another.

ALEX. I actually think I just want to lie on the floor while you grate cheese into my mouth.

He laughs.

JESSE. Gruyère?

ALEX. Sure.

JESSE. I've got a sharp little cheddar in the pantry...

She laughs.

ALEX. The pantry?

Smiles.

Eye contact.

Beat.

I am so in love with you.

JESSE. So stay...

ALEX. That has never –

She pulls herself up.

Picks up a Modern Israeli phrasebook from the dresser...

Why are you learning Hebrew?

He takes it, puts it back.

Where are you moving to?   JESSE. Please stay.

I can't stay.

JESSE. Then I'm coming with you.

ALEX. I'm not sure I want you to.

JESSE. Please don't take Poppy away from me.

ALEX. There is this...

This. Panic... in you.

This fear. This fury.

And it's inexplicable. And it's terrifying.

It's poisonous, Jesse.

And I saw it from the moment I met you.

JESSE. I'd just had the shit beaten out of me in fairness…

ALEX. And I wanted to –

Not save you… not that exactly. But try and find a way to make it better.

JESSE. I just need you with me.

Everything is better when you're with me.

ALEX. And that's all I have ever tried to do.

Just make it better for you. Lighter.

The big stuff – love, our marriage… guidance and all the big-changey relationship stuff.

JESSE. It's a two-way thing.

We both have –

ALEX. But little stuff too.

Making sure we have your favourite food.

Folding your clothes.

That's all so domestic – I'm not your wifey…

JESSE. Alex, I –

ALEX. No Jesse. It's my turn to talk.

I've tried to care for you… really care for you… I've tried to make you laugh and make sure there's been intimacy and love and happiness and celebrations and parties, dinners, sleeps, sex, mornings, movies…

Music. That's always been our thing. I know you don't give
a shit about it as much as me, but you go along with it, and
we have all these memories, this life we built... – telling you
I love you in a helicopter just above Liberty Island, those
crazy Thai massages after the Full Moon Party, floating in
the Dead Sea, Paris. New York. Hackney... Here.

And Poppy.

We made a person... Jesse.

We built an actual life.

And I have to protect her.

JESSE. This is exactly my point.

ALEX. From you.

JESSE. Whoa.

ALEX. This fear in you is just too too much... it's ruined you.

It's ruined us.

I'm not going to let you ruin her.

JESSE. That is really unfair. It's every –

ALEX. Have you ever considered for a second that the only
person who hates you, that the only person who has ever
wanted to hurt you, is actually just you?

JESSE. I'll fight you for her. I will.

ALEX. And have you ever just considered that I'm not
responsible for that idiot in the park. Or the Spanish
Inquisition, or the bombing in Paris or Nazis or Hamas or the
Labour Party or any of it.

JESSE. Don't you think for a second that I won't fight you for
her.

ALEX. It happened. That's it.

JESSE. It keeps on happening.

ALEX. You can't let it define you.

JESSE. It defines me. There's scar tissue in my DNA.

ALEX. Well, I can't keep fighting it.

   I don't have the energy.

JESSE. There's scar tissue in her DNA too.

ALEX. No, Jesse. There's not.

JESSE. What does that mean?

ALEX. I'm not sure she is yours.

   I'm sorry.

   Beat. It instantly breaks him but he pulls it back.

JESSE. I don't care. I don't care. I don't fucking care.

   It's probably better. I don't care.

   I love her. I don't care.

   I love you. I love – just don't…

   This is everything.

   It's all…

   Beat.

   Please don't break it.

   Please don't do this to me.

   Long beat.

ALEX. All I have ever wanted is for you to stop being so
   frightened.

They just stare at one another.

I'm sorry.

She leaves.

He is destroyed.

2004. The beach terrace at Space Nightclub, Ibiza

The sun is coming up.

ALEX *is building a spliff. She's in generic boho-chic-beach party wear. She has a takeaway coffee cup.*

JESSE *walks in. Torn jeans and a dirty white T-shirt with the word 'Newport' emblazoned across it in the style of the Nike logo and swoosh. He also has a takeaway coffee cup.*

They're both a bit fucked, and a bit rough for it. Slightly smeared eye make-up and slightly dirty clothes.

It's been a very long, but equally very fun night.

JESSE *watches* ALEX *for a bit…*

She clocks him. Nods.

JESSE. So… What did you come as?

ALEX. Slightly Judgemental Shoreditch Twat.

　　You?

JESSE. Ironic Townie.

ALEX (*raises spliff*). Salut!

JESSE (*raises coffee cup*). Chin-chin motherfucker.

ALEX. British?

JESSE. Oggy oggy oggy!!

　　Oi oi – (*Filters off.*)

　　She's not impressed.

　　I obviously think those blokes are dicks.

ALEX. Obviously…

JESSE. You?

ALEX. I'm the promoter… summer season…

JESSE. So what brings you here?

ALEX. Any chance to torment slightly geeky boys at beach
    clubs in Ibiza, really…

JESSE. Well done.

ALEX. Chin-chin.

JESSE. But really…

ALEX. Getting fucked off my head on shit drugs and dancing to
    shit house music.

    You?

JESSE. Basically the same.

    Lads' holiday…

ALEX. You're a child.

JESSE. So are you.

ALEX. I DJ'd before.

JESSE. Bullshit!

ALEX. Nine to ten.

JESSE. p.m.?

ALEX. No. I'm just hardcore.

    He's working out the maths.

    Yes.

    p.m. Warm-up shift.

    The guy who owns the bar wants to fuck me. So let me have
    a go.

    Not a chance. By the way.

    So how is Club 18–30. Pulled yourself lots of – birds?

JESSE. Have you seen me?

ALEX. I have…

JESSE. Less Club 18–30 more Club three friends who are woefully unprepared for this...

ALEX. Why?

JESSE. Because we never leave Highgate.

It's like a posh prison

ALEX. Are you posh?

JESSE. Firmly middle.

Dad just lucked out when weird rich uncle who no one else liked died... so –

Ching. Ching. Ching. Deposit...

ALEX. Nice.

JESSE. Are you posh?

ALEX. No. I'm cool.

JESSE. I can tell.

She has finished making the joint. She presents it...

ALEX. Smoke?

JESSE. Weed?

ALEX. No. PG Tips.

JESSE. Here?

It's all in the look from her: 'Where else?'

Won't we get kicked out?

ALEX. You care?

JESSE. I care if we get arrested and deported and I get chucked out of college.

ALEX. Ah... now I understand...

JESSE. I don't know what that means.

ALEX. How do you say?

Drama Queen...

JESSE. Just like that. Perfect.

ALEX. We're fine. I'm the DJ. So, you don't want to smoke?

JESSE. Maybe down on the beach...

ALEX. They might not let you back in.

JESSE. Do you care?

ALEX (*shrugs*). My friends left hours ago...

JESSE. Mine didn't come...

ALEX. So what have you been doing all night?

JESSE. I scored some shit pills that I initially thought might actually be speed but now that they stopped working I think were probably just Pro Plus.

ALEX. And, what have we got in there?

JESSE. Double-shot mocha...

ALEX. Why?

JESSE. It's the only actual drugs I could get anywhere and we're on a boat tour to Formentera in about an hour... What you got?

ALEX. Smirnoff Ice.

JESSE. Smirnoff Ice?

ALEX. Smirnoff Ice.

JESSE. Why have you got Smirnoff Ice in a coffee cup?

ALEX. Habit.

JESSE. That doesn't answer the question.

ALEX. I enjoy Smirnoff Ice, it brings up the pills and when I have my coffee cup I want people to look at me and think, that girl...

... she's important.

Oh I bet she's off to a meeting.

Oh I bet she's off to the post office.

JESSE. I feel like right now people look at you and think oh I bet that girl's off her face on pills.

ALEX. I can neither confirm nor deny your allegations.

JESSE. So do you have any?

ALEX. Had.

JESSE. I've never taken an E.

ALEX. Don't.

JESSE. Why?

ALEX. It wouldn't end well.

JESSE. I can handle an E.

ALEX. You can?

JESSE. Abso-fucking-lutely-not.

ALEX. I don't think I can either.

I've been secretly cutting my hair every time I take it.

JESSE. Who you keeping it secret from?

ALEX. Me.

Ssssh…

JESSE. So don't take it.

ALEX (*considers*). Done.

Smiles. He does not know what to do with her…

What now?

JESSE. Enjoy working here?

ALEX. Medium.

JESSE. Just medium?

ALEX. Well I'm on the terrace talking to you and coming up like a twat so I'm obviously not taking it that seriously... What do you do?

JESSE. I'm at drama school in London.

ALEX. Taxi!

He smiles.

JESSE. You can't go...

ALEX. Why?

JESSE. This could be significant...

ALEX. How?

JESSE. The game-changer.

ALEX. Oh really?

JESSE. Yeah man.

We met at the beach.

We travelled the world.

Married. Kids. The whole shebang.

ALEX. Ah – you're a romantic...

JESSE. I just need ten seconds and you'll fall completely in love...

ALEX. Okay.

Go...

JESSE. Okay.

Wait...

ALEX. What am I waiting for?

JESSE. How long is ten seconds?

ALEX. Eight... nine...

Does the Countdown *jingle.*

JESSE. And did it work?

Considers...

ALEX. I guess we'll see...

I like your necklace...

JESSE. Thanks.

It's my dad's and then his dad's and then his... and his...

He shows her – it's a really cute Magen David.

ALEX. It's pretty

JESSE. I mean I was going for something a bit more masculine...

ALEX. I never buy anything delicate.

I don't have that kind of life.

JESSE. What kind of life do you have?

ALEX. I have a –

– a very cool life...

What do you think of Ibiza?

JESSE. It's fine.

I hoped it would be cooler.

ALEX. You're on the wrong side...

JESSE. Apparently...

ALEX. San Miguel is pretty cool.

A little more arty.

JESSE. There are so many dirtbags down here.

I wish someone would just round them all up and ship them off to an island.

ALEX. I think this might be the island.

JESSE. It kinda smells.

ALEX. Ah yes.

The stench of Ibiza. It's famous… you know.

The end of all hope, alioli and piss.

JESSE. I kind of love it.

ALEX. Me too.

JESSE. Want to stay forever…?

ALEX. We'll see…

Beat.

JESSE. Wait…

ALEX. What?

JESSE. Listen…

They listen. Beat.

We hear 'Fuck the Pain Away' by Peaches/2ManyDJ's coming from inside.

Can you hear that?

Tune!

ALEX. I love this song. This song gives me goosebumps.

JESSE. I love M People.

ALEX. M People…?

JESSE. Do you get M People in Ibiza?

ALEX. We get M People in Peckham.

JESSE. My first dance with my mum at my Bar Mitzvah was to 'Movin' On Up'.

ALEX. You're Jewish…?

JESSE. Chosen. Yes.

You?

ALEX. I never get chosen for anything.

JESSE. I'd choose you.

ALEX. What for?

JESSE. What are you good at?

ALEX. This.

JESSE. So, I chose well.

ALEX. Who fucken knows...

How's chosen?

JESSE. It's potentially good you know... Israel are gonna
withdraw from the Gaza Strip and the West Bank... And
South Lebanon and loads of prisoners from both sides are
being freed and I dunno – it suddenly feels like a corner. You
know. A new dawn...

ALEX. Oh you're in to the politics?

JESSE. I'm not sure I am to be honest... but I hope that if they
get this right, in Israel... maybe everyone else will stop
coming for us... you know...

ALEX. Does everyone come for you?

Beat. Is about to. Stops.

JESSE. It's too boring. Let's talk about something else...

This promoting thing... you on your gap year?

ALEX. Yeah that's it...

JESSE. What?

ALEX. Do you know how much uni costs?

JESSE. I vaguely know how much drama school costs...

ALEX. I can't afford to go to university!

JESSE. Oh.

Shit.

ALEX. Yeah.

It's alright for some.

JESSE. Student loans…?

ALEX. It's fine. I have a plan.

JESSE. So what's the plan?

ALEX. Well if I tell you that, I'm gonna have to kill you.

JESSE. Please don't kill me.

Do you wanna go to uni?

ALEX. It's not all about uni.

JESSE. Do you want to though?

ALEX. I don't 'three K a year plus living costs' wanna go to uni…

JESSE. We could make that in a night…

ALEX. How?

JESSE. Three hundred paracetamol.

Tenner a pop.

Everyone's way too fucked to even notice…

ALEX. And here was I thinking you were a nice Highgate boy who wanted to go off and save the world.

JESSE. What the fuck ever gave you that idea?

ALEX. Don't all nice Highgate boys wanna go off and save the world.

JESSE. I mean mainly.

But. Fuck that.

Although if *you* wanted go off and save the world.

Then I'd totally come with.

ALEX. I haven't asked you.

JESSE. Please?

ALEX. Um.

JESSE. *Pretty please?*

ALEX. Okay. Sure. Yes.

But as the realist in the room...

JESSE. Beach.

ALEX. As the realist on the beach...

JESSE. Don't be a realist.

ALEX. Fuck it.

Done.

Let's totally go off and save the world.

JESSE. Good...

Cos you know it probably starts with us...

ALEX. You and me us?

JESSE. Why not?

ALEX. Why the fuck not...

JESSE. And we could still sell the paracetamol to fund the plan
so –

Win-win.

Beat.

What you looking at?

ALEX. Just thinking...

JESSE. About...?

ALEX. What's your name?

JESSE. Jesse. What's yours?

ALEX. Alex.

Beat.

JESSE. Hi Alex.

ALEX. So… Jesse…

Do you wanna go smoke this spliff and get off with me?

THREE

Introduction
Stephen Laughton

In truth, I'm still not sure if *Three* will ever see the light of day in a theatre; we plan to perform it in early January 2019 but, as I write this at the end of November 2018 and reflect on the last few months, it still feels like a long time off – anything could still happen.

I wrote this short play in response to the kidnap and murder of Naftali Frankel, Gilad Shaer and Eyal Yifrah in 2014. I won't go into why, or how it affected me – it just kind of did. I had been wanting to write some kind of response to *Seven Jewish Children* by Caryl Churchill – a lot of Jewish writers have, or have wanted to – and this event just resonated with me. I think now, four years later, we are still feeling the implications of that murder, of the war it started. I wrote *Three* in a kind of homage, certainly following the style of *Seven Jewish Children*.

One of the things that stopped me writing a response to that play before was, mainly, a thought that I couldn't quite shift, still cannot shift, that still challenges me, namely: who the hell am I to take on our greatest living playwright? No one, actually. Just a lad in a room with all the feelings both the play and this particular incident threw up. And that's all I ever am… so why not?

I'm not going to criticise *Seven Jewish Children*. It's what theatre should be: beautifully written and confronting. I'm glad the original production was made with a Jewish team. It's problematic, sure – not necessarily just the play itself actually, but the title is naughty; it conflates Jews and Israel. If we're ever going to actually tackle modern anti-Semitism, we have to pull that apart. We diaspora Jews are no more responsible for what happens in Israel than any other person on the entire planet who doesn't get an Israeli vote. And that runs into billions.

For the record, I am horrified by the blockades and the settlement building and the brutality. But, I'm also a romantic

Zionist. I feel a very deep connection to the land. I also feel like I can want a Jewish homeland and I can also want a safe Palestinian homeland and respect for the Palestinian people.

I digress. I don't want to be drawn too far into politics in a short introduction to a short play.

I think the other problem with *Seven Jewish Children* was the controversy it caused. Still now, nine years later, it remains upsetting. We planned to read both *Seven Jewish Children* and the following response piece, *Three*, after the performance of *One Jewish Boy* on 15 December. The outcry, the force and the fury was tangible. Scary, actually. I've had a crazy time since we announced the play in August. We've had to be in contact with Community Security Trust (CST), a Jewish security company who deal with threats and the like. I've had anti-Semitism – a lot of anti-Semitism actually – thrown at me. The title alone, *One Jewish Boy,* became a target; then we had to create a new poster because the old one kept getting destroyed. I've been accused of blowing up Palestinian children, been called an enabler, held to account for a whole host of issues that I not only have nothing to do with, but hate from the depths of my soul. And not once, in any of these attacks did anyone once check in. It was all based on assumption and, mainly, the use of the word 'Jewish' and its relationship to Israel or Palestine. Lest we forget – assumption is the mother of all fuck-ups.

I've literally, actually, in fact, had each of the four pillars of anti-Zionism – blood libel; power/money; split loyalty/untrustworthiness; Israel – aimed squarely in my direction from both sides of the political spectrum over the past few months. And when you add that to the rise of anti-Semitism that inspired me to tackle this play in the first place, I'm going to admit that there are times when I have been scared. It comes from all sides: young and old, right and left and even some very upset Jewish people getting equally furious with me because of my political beliefs, my stance against blockades and settlements in Israel and the sheer fact that I wanted to discuss *Seven Jewish Children*. Even some of the friendlier organisations with whom I have years-long relationships have tried to strong-arm me into censoring the Churchill play. And that's sad. If we cannot discuss these issues, how can we move past them? There are moments when it has felt tough. But nothing meaningful is easy, right?

The current plan, at the time of writing, is that on 5 January 2019 we'll hold a vigil for peace after the performance of *One Jewish Boy* that will contain some readings. I'm scared about including *Seven Jewish Children* within that – there have been threats from both sides of the argument. This is not cowardice on my part – I'm a political artist and I'm happy to put myself on the line and take this. If anything, it shows we're confronting something important. But I'm not the only person here, and I still have a responsibility to my team, my hosts.

I plan to read *Three* though, and to discuss *Seven Jewish Children*.

There are no 'directions' for *Three*; it can be read by ten people; it can be read by a hundred. On the 5 January 2019, I plan to read it alone.

December 2018

1

Tell your mom I love her

Tell yours

Tell her she'd get it

Don't piss him off

Tell her she's well fit

Don't tell her that!

Tell him we need to get home

Tell him I'm trying

Tell him we should hitch

You tell him

Tell me the time

Yeah tell me the time

Tell him Brazil are playing Croatia

Tell him to stop complaining

Tell him it starts tonight

Tell him I know

Tell him we're gonna miss it

Tell him there's a time difference

Tell each other!

Tell him that car stopped

Tell him to talk to them

And to hurry up

And that there's three of us

Tell him to shut up.

Don't tell me that

Tell him to run ahead

Tell them where we're going

Tell him to stop

Tell him they have guns

Tell him to run

2

Tell him I'm hurt

Tell him I know

Tell him I'm bleeding

Tell him they'll hear us

Tell him I can't see

Tell me what to do

Tell him to be brave like his brother

Don't piss him off

Tell him he taught me how to stop the bleeding

Don't talk about my brother

Tell him I'll stop the bleeding

Tell him I'm scared

Tell him we'll be out of here soon

Tell him we shouldn't have been hitchhiking

Tell you what… be quiet

I have a plan

Tell him the plan

I'll tell him in a minute

Tell him now

I'll tell him in a minute

Tell him it's too late

Tell him they're coming

Don't tell him that

Tell him they've seen us

Tell him to shout for help

Tell him not to

Tell them we're Jewish

Tell him they know

Tell him they're here

Don't tell them that

Tell him to put his hands in the air

3

Don't say anything

Don't say your name

Don't say where you live

Tell them about Koby

Don't give them ideas

Tell them they're in trouble

Don't piss them off

Tell them we can help

Tell them it's the Sabbath

Tell them I'm American

Don't

TELL HIM TO SAY SOMETHING

Tell him I'm thinking

Tell him yourself

Tell him there's a way out

Tell him I saw it on the way in.

Tell him there's just one guard

Tell him they have guns

Tell him I know

Tell him it won't work

Tell him it will

Tell them about shever and tikkun

Tell them we'll forgive them

Tell them nothing

No. Tell them it's war.

And tell them there are no virgins

That it's a lie

Don't piss them off

4

Tell them it's been days

Tell them we've had enough

Tell them I'm tired

Tell them I'm hurt

Tell them we're just kids

Tell them I'm hungry

Tell them I'm thirsty

Tell them you need the toilet

Tell them you're in pain

Tell them it's broken

Tell them they'll pay for this

Tell them I give up

Tell them we're sorry

Don't

Tell them I have brothers

Don't

Tell them we didn't do this

Don't

Tell them we did

Don't

Tell them we'll do anything

Tell them we have money

Tell them to stop hurting me

Tell them we work hard

And we're clever

And we can help

Tell them nothing

Tell them they're wrong

Tell them we were here first

Don't tell them that

Tell them we're accidental settlers

Tell them we'd like to share

Tell them we're sorry

Don't

Tell them it's gonna be okay

Tell them it wasn't us

Tell them it's a mistake

Don't

Tell them this is our home

Don't

Tell them we were driven out

Tell them we came back

Don't

That they attacked us first

Don't

Tell them we took our land back

We will keep taking our land back

Tell them the world will be looking for us

Tell them we have guns

Bigger guns

Tell them we won all the wars

Tell them we'll win this one

Don't tell them that

Tell them they can make a change

Tell them they can break the cycle

Tell them they can be the good guys

Tell them the Teffilah Zakah

Don't

Tell them please…

Tell them it hurts too much

Tell them I'm frightened

Tell them when it's over

I'll come looking for them

Tell them I will

Tell them I promise

Tell them they'll be sorry

Tell them I'm gonna fuck them up for this

Tell them it's just the beginning

Yeah. Tell them he's a hero

Tell them they'll die for this

Don't piss them off

5

Please tell them to stop hurting me

6

Ask them for some food

You ask

Ask them for a drink

Ask them how long

Ask them if we can watch TV

You ask

Ask them if we can go to the toilet

Ask them if we can call home

Just once

Ask them why

Ask them what we've done

Ask them why us

Of all the kids

Ask them why

Ask them nothing

Ask them if they have kids

Don't ask them that

7

Tell him not to be frightened

Tell him to be quiet

Tell him we'll protect him

Tell him god will

Tell him he's too loud

And it will be over soon

Tell him about that time in camp

Remember

Tell him how we sneaked out

Tell him how we did it together

Tell him we can do it again

Tell him we'll win

Don't

Tell him there's not many

Tell him we're heroes

Don't tell him that

Tell him we're leaving

Tell him to keep quiet

Don't frighten him

Tell him we love him

8

Tell him to stop screaming

Tell him they do it more when he's screaming

9

Tell them it wasn't me

Tell them I didn't know

Tell them I'm just a boy

Tell them I never hurt anyone

Tell them I like to read

Tell them I play with their children

Tell them it hurts

Tell them they're going too fast

I'm going to fall

Tell them they're hurting me

Tell them I'm innocent

Tell them I'm scared

Don't tell them that

Tell them about that time I found one of their boys and he
was hurt and I helped him and I gave him water and my T-shirt
because the sun was burning and the guns were loud and
I protected him and he thanked me

Tell them he was scared

Tell them he was young

Tell them I saved him

Tell them I'm a good boy

Tell them I'm good

Tell them I just want to go home

Tell them I won't say anything

Tell them I promise

Tell them I can't see

Tell them they don't have to put that over my face

Tell them I can't breathe

Tell them I can't breathe

Ask them

Please

Tell them I'm scared

Tell them not to take you away

Tell them no

TELL THEM NO

Tell them not to do it

NO

Tell them the bang hurts my ears

Tell them you were my friends

My brothers

TELL THEM

…

Tell them I'm just a boy

Tell them I don't deserve it

Tell them they're cowards

Tell them they're monsters

…

Tell them I'm sorry

…

Tell them I don't care any more

Tell them they were my brothers

Tell them I'll miss them

...

Tell them just do it

...

Tell my mom I love her

A Nick Hern Book

One Jewish Boy first published in Great Britain in 2018 as a paperback original by Nick Hern Books Limited, The Glasshouse, 49a Goldhawk Road, London W12 8QP

Cover image by Alex Fine Photography

Designed and typeset by Nick Hern Books, London
Printed and bound in Great Britain by Mimeo Ltd, Huntingdon, Cambridgeshire PE29 6XX

A CIP catalogue record for this book is available from the British Library

ISBN 978 1 84842 815 7

Woodland
CARBON
www.woodlandcarbon.co.uk
NICK HERN BOOKS
Printed on Carbon Captured paper